NO ONE ELSE CAN SEE YOUR FIRE

TREVOR BEAMAN

THE
SELF
PUBLISHING
AGENCY

Trevor Beaman
No One Else Can See Your Fire

Book Design | Petya Tsankova
Editor | Tara McGuire
Author Portrait Photography | Thesis & Henry Cromett
Cover photo | Jeremy Bishop on Unsplash
Publishing Management | TSPA The Self Publishing Agency, Inc.

For Eleanor and Benjamin

CONTENTS

INTRODUCTION

I wrote this book because I felt that the world was missing a voice of recovery and hope from someone who has lived through it all. I had war heroes, academic geniuses, and athletic figures I could look to for inspiration, but I couldn't find a trauma survivor who spoke to me as a man, husband, and father.

I have tried to write this book for close to twenty years. After the Stella Ganglion Block (SGB) injections and ketamine infusions I received in 2021, I finally had the ability to make this book happen. I want to share my story because I believe that sharing stories helps humans recover from their traumas. My story can spark change and build an understanding of what trauma does to you and the people around you. A driving force was seeing the impact of telling my story to other humans by being vulnerable, open, and transparent about all the ways trauma has impacted my mind, body, and soul.

From the moment I was born, I had the feeling that the deck was stacked against me. My family was torn apart by divorce, poverty, pride, dishonesty, and shame. Yet, perseverance was strong among my family members. My mother and father worked hard to provide for their children. However, sexual abuse, suicide, drug and alcohol abuse, depression, and attempted murder are all layers in the depths of my hell.

The book covers forty years of experiences and a lot of introspection about the past, present, and future. I don't think a person can forget the past. I don't think the human brain can simply stay in the present moment. I believe that humans will always think about the future, either being good or bad. I hope for good thoughts, but I know that is not realistic. Being human equals pain. Pain is part of the human experience. It took me thirty-five years to generate this idea in my own mind. I had been to therapy where this idea was spoken to me. I heard the message, but it didn't compute.

This book covers many types of traumas: drug and alcohol abuse, suicide, self-destruction, and the lowest depths of hell of living in my own mind. Each of these stories shows how certain events developed the way I see humanity. I write about the impacts of the choices of myself and others.

You will recognize that you are not alone in your pain. The path of recovery is painful; it will very likely be long and demand hard work. Your recovery is yours and no one else's. You decide what works best for you.

Trauma will never go away by stonewalling. Trauma will always come back at your lowest lows. Trauma is never as painful when life is going well. Trauma loves to compound on the bad, add to the shit show, and then create a dumpster fire. Remember that no one else can see the fire. You must be willing to open up. Other people will help you. Other people will care for and love you when you can't. This has been true throughout my life.

You must develop the skills to defeat the trauma and give yourself a fighting chance against yourself. You must not measure trauma. It's a biological response to living. The pain of life always leads to growth. You must always be growing in your life and looking towards the future.

CHILDHOOD

Never Safe

I was born on an early autumn day in 1980, in South Bend, Indiana. My birth was my first trauma. My mother had to have a C-section because I was breech. This made it impossible for my father to witness my birth. When I was growing up, my mother said that my father mentioned to her that he didn't see me born. I was the second boy and the last child that my parents had together. My parents had purchased a piece of land outside of South Bend. My mother and father lived there for two years before they got divorced. My brother Shawn was born fifteen months before me.

Ever since I can remember, my mom never had anything good to say about my father. My brother and I were constantly reminded that our father was unkind and that he physically and mentally abused her. My mom felt the need to get my brother and me away from that environment. This is the way I started to think about my father. Because of the stories she told me, I believed my father was an angry man. I heard about infidelity and physical abuse, but I never got any straight answers on what happened between my mother and father.

I was three years old when my mom, brother and I lived in the projects in South Bend. I slept on a mattress on the ground; there was no bed frame. When I picked up my blankets, cockroaches ran out from under the covers. These run-down apartments were now home. Public housing provided homes for families on welfare. My brother and I were the only white kids that lived in this neighborhood. While living in poverty, my mother finished nursing school. She continuously worked to provide my brother and me with a better life, or at least a better place to live. She was very focused on being a provider for the family.

My mom needed to get childcare for her kids. Being a student and on welfare, she didn't have the money to hire a sitter. Somehow, my mother met a man that wanted to help her take care of her children. I don't think that my mother had to pay for the time that this man would watch us. Being so hyperfocused on finishing school, my mom may have lost her motherly instincts to protect her children. We lived paycheck to paycheck, and she was not very financially literate, overspending and never saving money, living in the moment, and never thinking about the future.

My mother dated different men throughout my childhood, the worst of which was a firefighter who attempted to murder her in the house where we lived. I returned home from a weekend with my father. I walked into the upstairs master bedroom. On the top portion of the window to my right, there were holes in the glass. I looked past the holes and saw the neighboring house. Bullets had pierced through both homes. I felt scared and confused. I wondered if anyone was hurt. How could this happen? My mother explained that there was a disagreement, and her boyfriend attempted to shoot her with a shotgun. Then we went on living—no more conversation.

To make things worse, my mother made the choice to leave my brother and me at home alone at night when she went to work at the hospital. We were eight and six years old. Someone called child protective services. She worked the late shift from eleven p.m. to seven a.m. After this incident, my maternal grandfather moved in with us. My grandfather was a veteran of World War II. He had earned two purple hearts in combat. He was a hard man who liked rules and discipline. I don't remember if he ever laid on my brother or me, but he held himself in a manner that made me feel that if I got too far out of line, he wouldn't be afraid to discipline us. The dynamic of the house changed when my grandfather moved in. He offered more stability and structure than my mom could provide.

I have memories that are not just doom and gloom while I was growing up, and I have fond memories of my mother taking my brother and me to the beaches of Lake Michigan. I felt like we lived at the beach. I felt alive in the water. At this age, my brother and I looked like identical twins, with blonde hair and bronzed skin due to how much we played outside. We rode our Big Wheels and bikes all around the park, alone. We would climb the huge sand mounds, and we would spend hours running up and down this huge mountain of sand that was so hot it would burn our feet.

At the age of five, I started my love and desire to be surrounded by water. I love swimming and staying in the water forever. I visited the ocean a few times while I was growing up. The ocean offered a different feel to me. The waves were so much more powerful than in the lake. The ocean tasted different, and the salt would irritate my eyes and skin. The ocean was not as peaceful as the lake. The power of the current, the large waves, and the rip tides added a new experience, and I had to respect it. I knew that the ocean was more dangerous than the lake.

After two weeks of being with my mom, I would get a weekend with my father. He was a tall, fair-skinned man with dark hair and glasses, a cigarette smoker with an athletic build whose house seemed to be filled with clutter. His temper was a firecracker with a short fuse. He would throw and break things when he was upset. The times he would get upset scared me and were confusing for me to understand, but he never laid a hand on me or my brother.

His house collected trash, beer cans, and cigarette butts. The smell was like walking into a bar when it first opened. You can almost feel the smell about to hit your nose like it's physically touching you. I never really minded the mess and smell because I loved being with my father. He made me feel protected.

My father always seemed to take us to Pizza Hut when we visited him on his weekends. I can remember the smell of burning tobacco every time we got into my father's Jeep. He smoked Marlboro cigarettes, and the red and white hard box would be in the front pocket of his shirt. I can hear the flapping plastic that covered the outside of the frame of his soft-top Jeep. I can remember not because of the smell of the cigarettes or the noise of the plastic, but because of the song playing on the radio. It was 1986, and Robert Palmer's "Addicted to Love" was a big hit. This song seemed to play on the radio every time I was with my father. This song just spoke to me. I was six, and I loved the beat and the catchy hook. The words felt naughty, and I got the chills. I am sure this wasn't the first time I started to sing a song, but it was the start of me being emotional when I listened to music. Music, cigarettes, and pizza were common, and these moments provided normalcy. I knew what to expect, and I felt safe with my father.

My mother had been through different relationships with men, and I had seen the outcomes of violence. I didn't want her to be alone. I wanted her to have a family. Being a single mother raising two children on her own must've been difficult. My brother and I were hard to control. We were wild and did not behave. I lit fires, continuously played with fireworks and was mischievous. One of the worst things I did while living in South Bend was to throw rocks and bottles off of overpasses at cars. At this time, I was struggling in school; my toughest time was with reading and sitting still.

My soon-to-be stepfather arrived in South Bend when we lived in the projects. He had moved from the suburbs of Chicago to attend Holy Cross College. He said he opened an address book and prayed to God to give him guidance on where he should go and what he should do in his life. He flipped through the book of colleges that provided the path to becoming a priest. He said that he told himself that *God shall guide me to where I place my finger at random.* So, my soon-to-be stepfather packed his things in his car and moved to South Bend, Indiana. Still, to this day, I have no idea how he and my mother met.

As my soon-to-be stepfather entered my family's life, we started attending church. I went to first and second grade at Holy Cross Elementary School. I learned about God and the Bible and First Communion. My mother chose this school for us because it provided the best education she could afford. We went to church every weekend, but it seemed like more of a chore and a waste of time to me. I didn't have any connection to the church and its message; I went to church because I was told that I had to.

While I was in second grade, I took reading and math tests to see if I had a learning disability. I didn't struggle much with math, but reading, especially out loud, was very difficult. Reading on white paper seemed more difficult. In one technique, the teacher placed colored plastic sheets over the words on the paper. I felt that it helped me read better. I spent one-on-one time with a special teacher after the testing was complete. I was now removed from my normal classroom and placed in a different room. I wore colored-lens glasses which changed the color of the paper and seemed to help me read better. I felt that I was different; the colored-lens glasses made me stand out from my classmates, and I felt embarrassed to wear them in a classroom. My struggles at school were just a part of my problems. My at-home family life was about to be turned upside down.

With the attempted murder and the issues with protective services, my mother decided it was best for her to consider marrying my soon-to-be stepfather. This decision would make us move to Glenview, Illinois, where my soon-to-be stepfather had grown up. The drive was about three hours. I was picked up and put into a car, and we left. I hated that we left our friends, but I just didn't have a choice.

Glenview is a small, wealthy town in the northern suburbs of Chicago. There are golf courses and tree-lined neighborhoods that are beautiful to drive around. It's picture-perfect living. I wasn't lucky enough to live in those areas. I just got to see them as we drove by in the car.

We moved into a run-down apartment complex that included six or seven different buildings and townhouses. These buildings were red brick and never had enough parking spaces for the number of cars owned by the people living there. More people were living in the apartments than were supposed to. The apartment buildings were littered with broken doors; the latches of the screen doors never worked, and the doors were constantly being caught by the wind. Screen doors would slam shut at all hours of the day. That sound became normal.

The coin-operated washers and dryers sat in a room between the breezeway and the parking area. The lint smell of the dryer always stood out when I returned home. The walkways were all concrete and always dirty. The outside of the building looked run down; the white paint had grown moss, and green mold had grown up the siding. Most of the screens of the windows were missing, ripped, or hanging out on the windowsill. The apartment that we lived in had two bedrooms and one bathroom and was very cramped for four people. There was a small kitchen that always felt crowded, and we had a small, circular table that we ate at. In both bedrooms, there were water beds which took up much of the space. I stayed in the same room with my brother since we didn't have any space to ourselves.

Both our headboards had aquariums, and both aquariums had exotic geckos and the remains of dead crickets. The tub in the bathroom was short, and the total space was just tiny compared to where we had come from in the last house.

I started school there in the third grade. I was bigger and a year older than the other kids because my mother had held me back in kindergarten. I felt as if I didn't fit in with the other kids who had grown up through the previous grades together. I may have looked like I needed to progress because of my height and size, but I lacked the skills to advance to the next grade. My English skills were awful, and I had a hard time reading and spelling. I just couldn't make words appear in my mind when I was spelling and reading. Sounding out words just wouldn't work for me. Reading out loud was scary, and I avoided it at all costs. I would lose my place on the paper and speak words that I thought naturally came next. I stumbled and read slowly, and I felt that kids were making fun of me. Yet, I don't remember any kids ever saying that I was stupid or slow. The glasses that I had received in second grade didn't help me fit in with the other students, so I rarely wore them.

I struggled with reading out loud and with my comprehension. I had to read things over and over to get an understanding of what was trying to be communicated. I often became very frustrated with the amount of time it took me to complete assignments. I would be transferred to fourth grade in the middle of the school year. I struggled with the annual state testing, but I would move on to the fifth grade. The summer after my fifth-grade year became even tougher at home.

The other people in our neighborhood were poor Whites and Hispanics. Some of the people I knew and a few of my friends were members of a primarily Latino gang, the Latin Kings. The gang was just doing petty crimes and destroying common property. The gang members sold and smoked marijuana. At age nine, I started to see what poverty and street life provided. In the summer after fifth grade, I wanted to be one of the *boys*. I wanted to fit in. I was really looking for acceptance and to be a part of a group.

One day, I finally chose to be beaten or jumped into the Kings to become a shorty. A shorty is just slang for young kids who were members of the gang. I was pinned in a corner for two minutes while three older teenagers beat the life out of me. The following day, my back was covered with purple, red, and dark bruises. I couldn't hide these bruises. Even with the pain, I had a sense of belonging to something that was bigger than me, and that felt good.

Soon, my mother walked in on me taking a shower and

saw the aftermath of me getting beaten into the Latin Kings. My mother did what any mother would do—she called the sheriff. *Thanks!* Mom had no idea the way this crushed me because of the impact this would have on the streets with the other gang members. I was looked on as a rat or a snitch. My mother had no understanding of what respect in the streets meant; she wasn't a part of the neighborhood like I was. She just didn't understand what she had done to me. My mother and the sheriff asked me question after question. I felt like I was back in that corner of the kitchen. After an hour of pressuring me, my mother made me confess and identify the teenagers who had assaulted me. This confession did not go over well within the neighborhood. I would spend the next eight years looking over my back because of a choice I couldn't change. This was the first time I was scared that something seriously bad was going to happen to me outside of my home. This fear lived inside me for years.

My family moved again that summer, out of the apartments and into a trailer park across town. As you can imagine, the people my parents were trying to get me away from lived there, too. It was just another neighborhood that had poverty and gang members. I always wanted to be outside and wanted to make friends. I felt that people were always peering through windows when I was around. That summer, I had to go to court to be a witness to the assault. Yet, while I was at the courthouse, the lawyer that was prosecuting the teenagers for my assault told my mother that there was enough evidence of other crimes that my statement and charges wouldn't make a difference in their sentencing. I was sent home, and I never had to testify in court. I think this blessing helped me out. Maybe the lawyer understood more than my parents about the impact of me testifying in court.

My brother spent most of his time at home reading books and playing video games. The trailer park had thirteen streets, with the trailers placed six feet apart. People didn't have grass or yards, just a parking spot for your car and a plot of land to place the trailer. The double-wide trailer upgraded our status though. There were now three bedrooms, two bathrooms, and a much larger kitchen. The best part was that we finally had a washer and dryer in our home. We didn't have to go to the coin laundromat which made me feel poor. I started sixth grade living in this trailer.

I had the basic necessities to live, and I never felt as if I had to search hard for food. We didn't have to worry about the water being shut off. We were just living in the poorer part of town. I never felt that I was poor, but I was ashamed of where I lived. I lived in a place that grew hard people, people who were grinding through every day to live and provide for their families.

In sixth grade, I started playing football. I loved being part of a team and winning. My coach moved me into different positions up and down the offensive and defensive line. With my size, these positions made sense. I played the game well and was an asset to the team. During the games and practices, we were a team. When practice and the games ended, the kids went their separate ways in their white Range Rovers. I felt looked down upon by the other kids on the team because they knew where I lived, and I generally wasn't invited to the same after-school activities. I enjoyed playing football in middle school, but the desire to work out outweighed playing games.

Along with my struggles at school, in the neighborhood, and with sports, I was living another confusing dynamic that revolved around abuse. When I was eight years old, my stepfather started sexually abusing me at night while my mother was at work and my brother slept in the next room.

When the abuse started, it was kind and gentle, a very loving touch of laying close to me and rubbing my body. His hands gently glided over the skin on my chest. He caressed my face, chest, and legs, and eventually, he would find his way to my genitals. The enjoyment I felt when he rubbed and stroked my penis in a soft and caring way was the hardest part of the trauma. I was eight years old and being touched by someone felt good. I couldn't understand what was happening to me, or why, but I knew it was pleasurable. My brain craved the feelings and the hormone release that resulted from what was being done to me.

I kept my mouth shut about the abuse. I had a family, and I didn't want to lose that. I would hold hands with the man at church and other family gatherings. This man was raping me at night, but at the same time, listening to the Gospel and priests lecturing about kindness and humanity. As I sat in church and learned about God and religion, I had questions that didn't have any answers.

As time went on, my stepfather increased the length of the encounters, and he started to explore different areas of my body. I think I was around the age of ten. My stepfather would remove me from my bed at night, or I would sleep in my parents' bed. The gentle touching was over. Now, he moved straight into forcing my genitals into his mouth.

The abuse would leave my penis chaffed and sore for days.

I was so little that penetration to my anus couldn't happen, but with the use of lotions, I was forced to penetrate him. He would force his penis into my mouth. He would ejaculate on and around my face, in my mouth, and all over my body. I would lay still as he cleaned me up with tissues, and then I would fall asleep.

Feeling stubble and the smell of lotions are still triggers for me and bring these memories flooding back when I encounter them. These are the initial memories that would flood my mind later in life, memories I can't forget.

I never really knew when my stepdad was going to touch me. He arranged the time to get me alone with him so that he could take advantage of me. This monster worked at the conference and retreat center near our home as a bookkeeper and night custodian. There are many bedrooms for visitors, kind of like a hotel. At times, he would have me spend the night at his job alone. I am unsure how many times abuse happened there.

When the abuse started to happen outside of the home, I questioned his actions. I had become so accustomed to the sexual abuse that I accepted when he would fondle me while we were in the trailer. He would touch my body and make me touch his. He would lay next to me. I felt more like an "object" when the abuse happened outside of our home. When he would touch me outside the house, he seemed very distant. I knew when he suggested that I spend the night at the Towers, that he was going to rape me.

———

It was the winter of my seventh-grade year when I first attempted to commit suicide. Christmas provided me with many mixed feelings. The highs of being around a loving family and being out of school were coupled with the lows of the abuse I suffered.

I was alone in the trailer. I opened the medicine cabinet in my parents' bathroom that had a single sink, a plastic tub, and a large mirror, just a basic trailer bathroom. My stepfather took medicine to control his high blood pressure. I consumed two weeks' worth, plus a handful of aspirin and some other pain pills in a single gulp. All the pills rushed into my body. I filled the tub, removed my clothes, and looked at myself in the mirror. All I saw in my hazel eyes was sadness and pain, an exhaustion from living with all these memories. As I slipped into the water, my body felt warm, and I was comfortable. I had chosen a normal yellow Bic razor, which I slid side to side on my wrists. There was blood, and I was cut, but nothing like I had imagined.

I started to lose color in my skin, and my body was now reacting to the medicine I had swallowed. I thought this was going to be the end of my life. I had pictured the water dark red, and my pale body would be found lifeless. I wanted the pain in my brain to just stop. I cried, hoping everything would be over, everything gone.

The water got cold, and I put my clothes back on and emptied the tub. My mother found me, and being a registered nurse, she knew that something was not okay the instant she saw me. I was sitting on our couch in the living room. The lights were dimmed, and it was hard for her to see me. She asked me what I had done. I showed her all the pill packets I had swallowed. She made me drink milk of magnesia which made me vomit and continue to dry heave uncontrollably. Muscle spasms made my adnominal area exhausted.

While we drove to the hospital, I explained to my mother that I missed my father and that I didn't enjoy living in Glenview. As I drank water, I continued to throw up into a bowl and a towel on my lap throughout the forty-five minute drive to the hospital.

I was admitted to the hospital first before they moved me to the psych ward. My stomach was pumped, and the nurses gave me sixty-four ounces of charcoal and water to drink. The charcoal mixture was supposed to absorb all the drugs I'd taken. Every gulp I put in me just came right back up, and I was covered in a black mess.

Next, the nurses used a new method to try and get the charcoal to stay in my stomach. They ran a silicone flexible tube through my nose, past my throat, and into my stomach. The process was unpleasant but tolerable. As the nurse started to push the charcoal down the tube with a large syringe, it got clogged. The nurse pressed again with all her strength and instead of going down into the tube, all the charcoal sprayed throughout the room and on everyone's faces, like an artist throwing black paint at a white canvas. With a quick yank, the tube was out of my stomach and out my nose, a very odd feeling. The next try would be with a hard plastic tube through my nose. I felt it scraping the back of my throat on its way down to my stomach. Finally, all the ounces of charcoal somehow made it into my body.

The worst thing, other than my stepdad being at the hospital watching me for five days, was the charcoal that had to come out of me. This was the only time that I ever covered a toilet in a black mess.

I walked into the psychiatric ward, looked around, and thought to myself... *how in the fuck am I going to get myself out*

of here without telling the truth about why I tried to kill myself?
Then it hit me! Earlier that year, I was thinking about moving
back in with my father in South Bend. I had just found the
lie that everyone could believe, the lie that I could make into
reality. I would say that I missed my father, which was true,
but what I really wanted was for my stepfather to die. What
made the story more believable was that I spent a week in
the hospital, and my father didn't come to visit me.

My stepfather stayed next to me throughout my stay. I
knew why he was there, but everyone else thought he was
caring and doing "God's work." I cried, and everyone believed the perfect story.

When I went back to school after the suicide attempt, I
began seeing a school social worker. She had half of a corner office with a black couch and her desk. There were fidget
toys around the room that I remember playing with while I
talked to her. I went twice a week for an hour to talk about
how I was doing in school and how I felt. I offered basic answers and talked about how much I hated school. I would
spend most of my time talking about simple, everyday teenager stuff like not fitting in and living in the trailer park.
During seventh and eighth grade, the social worker helped
me get through some tough times. This began my therapy;
I was just twelve years old.

I knew I could convince people of whatever I wanted if
there was enough feeling attached to my words. I developed
a small prison in my mind and put a monster inside of it. The
mental prison was where I could put everything in my life, and
I was convinced it would never be let out. The monster grew
stronger over the years. The monster became a friend and
took care of me. My own mind hid all the pain and torture.

I was starting to learn many lessons about just how powerful my brain could be.

It was around this time that my own internal debate between "right" and "wrong" was constantly raging. This was also the time when my "never quit" or "you can't beat me" mentality took hold. I learned about the different faces I could wear to help mask what was truly going on inside. These disguises, these masks, only painted a portrayal of happiness, family, and love. These masks hid truths about the bad things that were happening. Most of the overwhelming thoughts that consumed me were about survival and making others happy.

———

Being a poor kid in a rich community made me want to work my ass off. A lot of the real learning I would use later in life was developed from the hustle of the streets and having nothing to lose. I learned how to survive, how to be a hard worker, and how to be needed. However, my family was more well-off than the people that surrounded us. Having a double-wide trailer was different and was a big deal, compared to many of my friends who were living in single-wide trailers.

The work ethic I have today is based on two things: survival and being dependable. I worked hard cutting grass when living at the apartments at age nine, and I worked at the Towers during the summer before seventh grade when I was eleven. I learned new skills and developed my self-worth. I loved being dependable. My word and my handshake were about all I had as I was growing up.

When I was in fourth grade, I started to work doing door-to-door lawn maintenance. It was hard work, and I did it alone.

I wanted to make people happy. I cared about my work and tried really hard to do a good job. I loved helping people even if they didn't pay. I loved being outside and working with my hands and body. I generally woke up before my alarm went off on the weekends and in the summer. I was on time for work. I knew that other people's time was valuable, and I tried not to burden others because I wasn't prepared. Repeated success builds a strong work ethic. Success in my early childhood helped me try new things that I might not have been good at initially.

The summer job at the convention center where my stepfather worked provided me with an off-the-books, cash-only job. I would work hard on the weekends picking up garbage left on the grounds by partyers in the park behind the building. I was eleven or twelve when I taught myself how to drive a manual tractor with a trailer. I would grind the gears and pop the clutch a lot as I practiced over and over. I lifted heavy trash bags into the trailer. I enjoyed the work even though the garbage smelled horrible and was gross. The smell took me back to being at my father's house full of trash bags of rotten food and empty beer cans. I was really excited to be getting paid for my time and earning money. I always looked for things that would provide me with my own independence from my parents.

While working as a young teenager, I started to make enough income to keep me from living a life of the rat race and debt. I got a worker's permit when I was fourteen. I started to work at a roller skating rink as a guard, concession person, and behind the skate rental counter. My stepfather's father worked in the repair shop, and I was always able to get the best wheels and bearings for my skates. I didn't make a lot of money, but what I did get was the ability to work late nights on Fridays. I stayed out late and even had the opportunity to drink alcohol near the end of the late shift.

The Playdium in Glenview attracted a rougher crowd, and this scene was something cool I was involved in. I sure could fly on those skates. The wind across my ears and the rolling of the wheels on the wood floor hummed in a manner that sent me to another world. Music really stuck when "Rapper's Delight" by The Sugarhill *Gang* was playing in the DJ booth. I knew I could use music to leave the world, the trailer park, my parents, gangs, being poor, school, the constant thoughts of wanting to die. Music helped me forget everything that my mind raced over. Music gave me a break from the pain I had inside.

In the fall of 1993, when I was thirteen years old, I was in a friend's single-wide, one-bedroom trailer smoking pot for the first time. The television had chrome dials on the right side of the black box. To help find the channels, a rabbit ear antenna was connected to the TV. The walls were covered in brown wood slatting and were paper-thin. Eazy-E was the CD spinning everywhere in my neighborhood. The album *It's On (Dr. Dre) 187um Killa* burned all through my soul. It was the only guide we had as misguided kids. "Boyz-n-the-Hood" was the song that played. The small inhalations I took were of mostly burning paper, and the marijuana was full of stems and very little buds. The small puffs seemed to fill my lungs fast. The smoke burned, sat in the back of my throat, and continually made me cough.

Eazy-E's music didn't make me want to hurt anyone, do drugs, or treat people badly. Eazy's music was easy for me to relate to, and I didn't feel as much of an outcast or abnormal in the poor neighborhood when I listened to it. The music was now connected to me. Marijuana made my head feel heavy, but my ears opened up and I really listened.

I didn't have my driver's license yet, but I was already tired of asking people for help. I wanted to be able to support myself so no one could ever tell me what to fucking do again. So, I would work at the Playdium on Friday nights and weekends. I would also work any birthday parties that got scheduled. Cash in hand provided me with more power than I ever had before. It was the first time I earned something that no one could take away from me. When I earned it, I didn't have to answer to anybody. *Fuck off, Mom and Dad! I'm ready just to be on my own.* I had more free time in the summers to work as many hours as I could. I didn't have a need for my parents to provide me with anything anymore. Having money was awesome, but working provided me with an escape from the horror film I was living in. Like school, a job was a place where I felt safe. That sick man who I was forced to live with did not surround me. A job provided avoidance from the abuse; if I wasn't around, then that life didn't exist.

A big next step for me was being confirmed. I was told that if I could complete the schooling and the Confirmation process, I would be looked at as an adult in the Church, and I could then choose whether to attend at all anymore. With the power of choice in my mind, I thought I would play the long hustle on my stepfather. I had zero hope that God existed, and I knew if he did, then he wasn't cheering me on. Plus, the whole God thing just wasn't making sense to me. If my stepfather could take advantage of me in a church, which was his place of employment, then my trust in God was destroyed.

I put in the hours and went to Sunday school each week. It took about a year to finish the process and be confirmed at Easter mass. I did all the work and never complained about going to Sunday school because I knew what the outcome would be. I would never have to attend church again. It would be my choice, and I would have the power. Having the ability to say no was very powerful to me. *Come and get these two middle fingers, God... Fuck you!*

———

During the summer of 1994, before my freshman year at Notre Dame High School in Niles, Illinois, I got a job at an equestrian farm. I learned how to take care of horses and the equipment needed to ride. I spent time discovering how to ride Western and English saddles. The Western has a horn in the front to hold onto or tie a rope to; English saddles do not have the horn in the front of the saddle. This job present-ed the hardest physical work that I had ever done. Throwing hay bales, feed, and cleaning stalls were all part of my job. It was dirty and exhausting, but there was always something to do and always a beautiful girl to take a glimpse of or fanta-size about while she was riding the horses.

The horses were beautiful, and so were the girls who rode them. This was the summer that I met my first real girl-friend. She and I spent time at the barn, and, when I had time off, we went on the simple kind of dates that thirteen-year-olds go on. We would go get hamburgers and go to the movies and talk on the phone for hours.

I really explored my thoughts more deeply when it came to my sexuality. I now started having a tough time under-standing who I was sexually. Due to my stepfather's abuse and the initial pleasure I had received from it, I wasn't sure if I liked men or women, or if I just liked being touched. This idea scared me for many years. I had anger inside me, but I learned how to mask it with a smile. My smile was a coping mechanism I would use for a long time.

——

I started my first year of high school at a new place with new kids. I chose to attend the all-boys Catholic high school called Notre Dame rather than Glenbrook South High School because of the trouble I had had with gang members. Some of the gang members were seniors at this time and wanted to stay out of school. It was nice to get away from the kids that made me look over my shoulder, but it also introduced me to a group of kids who had spent their whole education together. Again, I thought I didn't fit in.

School was very difficult. I felt as if I wasn't smart, and that learning did not come easily. I felt like I was always behind and continued to struggle with academics. I wasn't bullied, but I was meant to feel like an outsider. The things I had going for me were my smile and my larger frame. I played football, which helped me get my anger out, but I was often injured. I decided I would switch to volleyball the following year. The pain of my sports injuries only made me want to work to earn money instead.

I continued to work at the Playdium during my freshman year. I may have taken a friend's girlfriend. I'm not sure if they were dating, but he sure as hell thought they were. I would get bullied and get in a few fights. I never really fought back; I would just wait until gym class when I could beat them on the mats when we wrestled. Being the winner at sports rather than winning a physical fight seemed more effective. The cost of attending a private high school was just not practical.

In my second year of high school, I went to Glenbrook South, and I made it onto the Boy's junior varsity volleyball team. I could play the game of volleyball well, and I excelled in blocking the ball. I was always in the right place to jump in front of the net to block the opposing team's spiker. I enjoyed being on that team, but during the season, I found my dream job working at a hospital across the street from the school. I put in forty-hour work weeks by working twelve-hour shifts on the weekends, and the $10 an hour I got in 1996 was amazing. I saved my money and bought a car, a cell phone, car insurance, cigarettes, and gas. It all came from my hard work. One of the best parts about working in the hospital was the food. I worked in the kitchen, making trays for patients and cleaning pots and pans. This job allowed me to stay out of the trailer.

Since starting high school, I had begun to notice more changes in my body. Going through puberty, "the teenage changes", I grew taller and started growing hair on parts of my body. The abuse slowed down as I got older, from happening once or twice a week to once every few months.

I met some wonderful women during this time in the kitchen. These ladies would drive or take the train from the South Side of Chicago to work in the kitchen each day. They were Black ladies who shared their lives with me, and I listened to their stories. They loved to call me "Baby". They talked about their families and God and worked harder than any other people I have ever met. I know they truly loved me, and I respected them.

A man named Bob, a Black Vietnam veteran, worked the dishwashing machine. He was quiet but had a special presence. I felt that Bob had lived a tough life and was trying to figure out why humanity was so cruel. I always felt that his heart had been broken by something I couldn't understand at just sixteen. I respected and cared for the people at Glenview Hospital. I earned money. I earned power through hard work, and I was taught about respect.

I started to see the education that I was receiving during the day was not helping me learn the skills to become a worker. The skills I needed to be successful in the workplace, like showing up on time, doing good work, and being kind to others, weren't the lessons I was learning in school. I figured that if I got my diploma, very few people would be concerned about my GPA. Who I was as a person made a much bigger difference to me than how I performed in certain classes. Science and math had zero impact on who I was going to be in the future.

I have never been an outwardly angry person. I just never felt that being upset caused much good. Losing control was the last thing I ever wanted to do; my father had shown me that. Along with the abuses I was receiving from others, I would abuse myself in many ways by binge-drinking, fasting, smoking a lot of tobacco, and taking risks by driving fast. I started smoking cigarettes around this time to be rebellious and as an internal way to cause me pain. I felt as if I was burning the pain out of me by filling up my lungs with smoke.

I kept all the abuse and trauma in my high school locker. I would drive to school, smoke three to four cigarettes, slam my internal hate and grief into my locker, then walk away from it. I was living a life that had two identities, and I was trying to live them simultaneously; I left my scared and over-whelmed memories right there in my locker when I started school every day.

Staying on top of all my tasks, my upcoming weekend work, my volleyball practices, and my homework kept my mind and body so busy that I never had to deal with the real demon inside of me, but it never seemed to take a break or relax. From the moment I awoke and put my feet on the floor, my mind either thought about dying or about killing my stepfather. This lifestyle worked for me for a long time, and it was very difficult, but, at the same time, no one no-ticed either.

A few months after getting my job at the hospital, I met a girl named Rebecca; she had wonderful blue eyes, blonde hair that stretched down her back, and perfectly round cheek-bones. She was gorgeous and extremely smart. Rebecca was two years older than me and a senior in high school. She lived with her father in the nearby town of Niles. Her parents were divorced, and her mother had remarried and lived in anoth-er part of Chicago. I remember meeting Rebecca through a friend of a friend. I was introduced to her one night while working late at the skating rink for a sleepover. I was still picking up extra shifts at the skating rink while also working at the hospital. I was making good money; I had my car, and I was able to spend a lot of time with Rebecca. This was great because I didn't have to spend as much time at home.

Rebecca and I were each other's first encounter with true sexual intimacy. At first, touching each other reminded me of how I felt when I was eight and my stepfather would touch me in places that felt good. With Rebecca, it was different, of course, but the real difference was that I was a consenting participant, and I wasn't acting like I was asleep.

The moment we connected physically was perfect. This kind of intimacy felt normal, which took my mind back to all the abuse that had happened in the apartment. Rebecca had a waterbed, and the sound of water crashing against the headboard was familiar. There were great smells in the air, and the energy was beautiful. I felt love and a sense of being connected, not what my stepfather had been putting me through over the last eight years.

Once, while Rebecca and I were having sex at her house, I heard a loud pounding on her door. It was her father. I had a feeling he was going to put his shoulder through the door. Rebecca jumped up off the waterbed, and I can still recall the sound and feel of the sloshing water. She ran to the door completely naked and prevented her dad's intrusion into her room. Rebecca screamed to leave her alone! We were lucky not to get caught that day.

My stepfather was still molesting me while Rebecca and I were together. It was really confusing and weird, but it helped me clarify that I wanted to be with women. Sexual contact with a man just didn't feel right to me. Yes, I would have thoughts of being touched by my stepfather when I was with other women. Unfortunately, those feelings and thoughts will be with me for the rest of my life. The trauma of how it felt to be touched when I was very young is brought back every single time a human being touches me in a manner that is pleasurable.

These are the memories that would drive me to drinking and drug abuse. When I had sexual relations, I wanted to be drunk because it helped me not think about being touched as a child.

I am super grateful for Rebecca in my life. She offered me somewhere safe to be rather than at home. I would make the forty-five minute drive from my trailer in Glenview to her house in Niles, several times each week.

In early December, just after I had turned sixteen in September, my brother Shawn and I were on our way to a concert at (what was then) the Rosemont Horizon. We were two kids, excited to see Local H open up for Stone Temple Pilots, front and center in the mosh pit. Local H, a two-person band from nearby Zion, had some of the loudest drums I have ever heard. The bass shook every fiber of my being, and I loved it! Scott Weiland, the lead singer of STP, was absolutely extraordinary! Stone Temple Pilots played an electric, an acoustic, and then another electric set. The total showtime was over three hours, and it was the best show I had ever seen. I can remember looking into Weiland's eyes and feeling the pain he carried. Weiland's eyes were devil-red and bloodshot. He sang with all his heart, and his performance on stage was incredible. The experience of the music and the show made the pain inside me disappear.

Near Christmas, a horrible snowstorm hit Chicago while I was at Rebecca's mother's house. I called home and talked with my stepfather. He insisted that I return home and was adamant that I could not spend the night away from our house. The amount of pressure and pushback my stepfather gave Rebecca's mom, a Chicago police officer, raised some red flags with her. Rebecca's mom had a hard time trying to understand why someone was so against me staying overnight somewhere. My stepfather would end up coming to pick me up rather than making me drive my own car back home.

This moment was the start of my desire to say something about what was happening to me. I just needed the right push to put me over the edge. I felt a strong desire to ask for help for the very first time. The idea that something was wrong with my stepfather's actions was becoming more and more clear. The responsibility I felt to keep my family together was starting to fade. I knew that I could speak up about the abuse by my stepfather when I got enough courage to do so.

At some point, my stepfather started working as a hospice worker or caregiver of children with disabilities. Many of these children were affected by disabilities ranging from Down syndrome to autism. My stepfather worked with these types of kids for many years. I remember him being praised by the children's parents about how much their kids loved him. He got compliments for changing the behaviors of these struggling kids. Sometimes, I spent time around the kids in his care. Some wore diapers and had zero communication skills with either their voice or sign language. All the children he watched were boys. Our family became more and more involved with the families that my stepdad cared for, so much so that I was offered babysitting jobs when my stepdad was unable to provide help to the family, or if the family needed additional help with their child. Of course, I helped out and took the money.

One afternoon, I was watching a boy named Austin who was around the age of six. I was asked to give him a bath that afternoon. Austin had very few speaking skills and was low functioning. It was hard for him to take care of himself or get dressed on his own. I helped Austin get undressed and assisted him into the bath. I washed his body and cleaned his hair. I noticed Austin was playing with his penis while

I cleaned his body. There was a point when Austin looked at me, smiled, and giggled with joy. I had a huge fear that he had also been shown what pleasure can come from your body as a response to another human's touch.

I got Austin out of the bath and dried him off. I put clean clothes on him, played with him, and fed him dinner until his mother came home. The way that Austin acted was the way that I had felt inside, only I had the means to control my behavior and actions.

That day, I knew I had to make a change to what was happening to me and to other children without a voice. I found the courage to speak up for all the children who couldn't say, "Help me."

Later that year, my mother asked me a question that would change the course of my life dramatically. I was close to turning seventeen and still using the same bathroom where I had attempted to take my own life four years earlier. I had grown so much since then. The nights of being abused had an impact on my daytime life. I was tired all the time. My penis would be raw from what felt like hours of stroking and rubbing. I had black and purple circles under my eyes from being sleep-deprived. These symptoms were signs that my mother should have picked up on, because she was both a mother and an emergency room nurse.

As I got older, the abuse by my stepfather became less and less frequent, but I was afraid that he was abusing other children and therefore did not need me. One night, after the sun had already set. I was in my parent's room and was agitated by the thought that my stepfather was hurting other children. My mother must have finally noticed something. I was showing that I was physically upset, but for some reason, the question she felt compelled to ask me was, "Is your step-dad fucking you?"

My mom didn't really talk in this manner directly to me unless she was serious. To this day, my mother insists it was an angel who spoke to her and told her to ask me this question. I have my doubts about that now after being a father myself. My response was, "You finally asked me the right question."

At that moment, the weight of the last eight years was lifted. It seems as if I needed the correct question to be asked before I would be willing to share the abuse, despite the years of depression and my first suicide attempt.

My mother and I left the house and took a three-and-a-half hour drive around Glenview. It was dark, and the streetlights offered a glow to soften her interrogation. She asked questions of when and where. We discussed all the times I was touched, and the different locations like the church, the hotels, and the vacations. I revealed all the things my stepfather had done to me, his attempts to penetrate my anus, placing his penis in my mouth, and the hours of rubbing and masturbation. I did not spare any of the details with her. This release was cathartic for me, but horrific for my mother.

I had lived with the same images and memories for more than eight years, and that evening, I shared them all with her in a few hours.

It was a long night of conversations, explaining what her husband had done to me. The abuse happened at least a hundred times that I could remember. She believed every word I told her, and it felt good to finally tell her the truth. I could finally be me and finally be free. I was able to take a breath of air and come up from the depths of my hell.

My mother's recognition and validation of the abuse was a huge pivot point in my life. It could have gone many ways, but the outcome of the conversation between my mother and me would spark the path which I live on today.

She took me to the Glenview Police Department to start the prosecution of my stepfather. When I walked into the station, I felt nervous about talking to the police about sexual abuse. But I also felt very calm, and I was confident that someone was going to take me seriously.

The police took statements from me and my mother in a booking room with a table and two chairs. My mother and I were separated when I gave my statement. I was offered water and a tissue for my tears. Everyone I told my story to believed and trusted me. I remember the police officer being quiet while I talked. He was very supportive and kind to me. We talked for a few hours, though it was difficult to speak with a man about the abuse; I felt awkward and uneasy inside when describing what had happened to me to another man.

When my statement was complete and we had finished with all the questions, the police went to the trailer and arrested my stepfather that night. He was charged with the abuse and sexual assault of a minor.

After being booked, my stepfather wrote a complete confession of all the acts of abuse he had committed on me. He was charged with thirty-seven counts of child sexual abuse. He was put into a holding cell and eventually transferred to the county jail, where the judge set a $300,000 bond for his release. The next day, my mother filed for divorce.

His parents were able to come up with ten percent or $30,000 to get him out of jail. I think that he spent less than thirty days in jail before his bond was paid. I would spend the next two years in and out of courtrooms trying to put him in jail for what he had done to me.

I had a strong and persistent desire to find him and kill him while he was out on bail. I knew where he was living, just a three-hour drive away. Somedays, I fixated on these thoughts. But I just continued binge-drinking, working, and spending time with friends.

The summer before my junior year, my brother relocated to South Bend and moved in with our father. Shawn ended up having problems living with our father. They had a falling out due to rules and being home at certain times. My brother found a new place to live. He needed a car, and I had two. I gave my brother my extra car so he could attend school and drive himself to work.

My brother Shawn was never abused by our stepfather and never suspected that anything out of the ordinary was happening to me.

After my stepfather was arrested, I still had to finish high school. My mom and I went to talk to officials at Glenbrook South High School to relay the information about what our family had been through. My guidance counselor, a very honest woman, shared her thoughts about my future. She said that she didn't see much of a future for me in higher education and that she believed I wouldn't live past the age of twenty-one. My mom didn't know how to respond to these comments; we were just trying to figure out how I could get through high school at the fastest rate possible.

My grandfather had just passed away in our home, my mother's ex-husband was in jail for molesting her son, and her oldest son had just moved out. This conversation with the counselor was the least of my mom's problems. I think that the counselor had this perspective due to the history of abuse and where we lived in the city. The trailer park kids did not have a great reputation for graduating. Most of my friends no longer attended the school. Most were kicked out of school, and others were in jail for attempted murder.

I was introduced to a psychologist who would be my second therapist. I went weekly to a very nice office in the nearby town of Highland Park, a very wealthy suburb with no trailer parks in sight, just Ferrari dealers and white Range Rovers. I remember his office was on the second story. He had a white beard and glasses and was well-groomed. He dressed in simple slacks and collared shirts. He had a Nantucket vibe, like he was going sailing after our meeting. Yet, talking to a man about what I had been through was difficult for me to do. I just didn't want to describe the abuse to him. The words made me feel embarrassed. We discussed the physical sexual abuse, but I never got too deep into how it made me feel.

Despite the counselor's opinion, we were able to come up with a plan that would allow me to graduate early from high school. During senior year, I would attend classes in the morning, then, after lunch, I would attend classes at an alternate school for kids who were trying for their GED. Many of the kids at the alternate school were my friends who were also struggling and had been kicked out of high school for drug or academic reasons.

I continued my relationship with Rebecca. We spent most days and weekends together when I was not at work. I went to her senior prom and watched her play basketball for her school. I enjoyed our time together, and I felt that we were very connected. She would go on to college while I was still a senior.

While I was at the alternate school, I took extra exams and reading assignments to help my friends who struggled to complete their daily work. They were either high, or they just could not stay on task to get anything done. During the last semester, I lived alone in the double-wide trailer. My mother had moved to Lafayette, Indiana, to work at a hospital there. My brother was in his freshmen year at Purdue University, which is in West Lafayette, Indiana, but he lived in the dorms. Our mother rented a small two-bedroom home with a detached garage across town.

All I had was a twin mattress without a bed frame and my car. I still can't understand how it was considered a great idea for eighteen-year-old me to live alone in the trailer. I had parties all the time, and my friends punched holes in the walls.

When Mom came for a visit, she wasn't pleased with the three garbage bags full of beer cans and the place destroyed. I'm not sure what she expected out of me at that point. I just didn't give a fuck about my future or my life. I would drink a six-pack of beer every night and work on homework. I lived all alone in the same trailer I had been abused in since I was a boy.

I was one of seven people in my class who would graduate from high school in January 1999. The other six were outstanding students in areas I didn't even know existed. These kids took AP classes, had 4.00++ grade point averages, and completed college courses. I didn't do any of these things and had a GPA of less than 2.5. I felt like I didn't belong at the ceremony and shouldn't have been graduating; I had hustled and cheated the education system. I wasn't supposed to be there.

I scored an eighteen on my ACT, which is on the low end of the average range. Still, I applied to Purdue, where my brother was already a student. Soon, I received a rejection letter from Purdue. However, that didn't stop me from moving to Lafayette after graduation. My mother had sold the trailer, so I moved in with her. I stayed a few months with her, but I needed to be out on my own. I moved into the fraternity where my brother was a member for the summer. He had rushed in the fall of 1998.

Rebecca and I broke up when I moved to Lafayette. However, she came to visit me at Theta Xi Fraternity that summer. Back then, Theta Xi Fraternity was in an area known to everyone at Purdue as "the acres". The house sat in the northern corner of campus, just west of the football stadium. We spent some time together, but I was not looking for kids and marriage the way she was. The thought of having a family, and the enormous responsibility that would bring at eighteen years of age, was terrifying. I was still trying to figure out what the hell had happened to me as a kid. I was in no way ready to start raising children of my own. In many ways, I was still a kid myself, an eight-year-old kid who was trying to figure out college life, alone.

I almost gave up trying to get into the University. As a last resort, I walked into the bursar's office with another member of Theta Xi. We found someone who could answer my questions, and I asked what I needed to do to be admitted. Surprisingly, the woman came back to me with a plan. She told me that I would need to enroll at Ivy Tech, a community college with a campus in Lafayette, take three summer courses there, and get at least a 2.0 so the credits could transfer over to Purdue. She also enrolled me in COM 214 at Purdue that summer, which was the basic communication and public speaking course.

From May until August, I attended both Ivy Tech and Purdue. I took an English course and two computer courses at Ivy Tech. It was a long and challenging summer especially since the pressure was on me to do well. I needed to maintain that "C" or better average for those transfer credits and to prove that I could handle the rigors of student life at Purdue. I passed two of the three classes I took at Ivy Tech. Of course, I struggled in English, and I failed that course. The two courses I passed would transfer over to Purdue, and I got the "C" I needed in the COM 214 class I took at Purdue.

In the fall of 1999, I rushed the Theta Xi Fraternity at Purdue University. Rushing is a term for the period when you are joining a Greek system in college. During the rush process, the brothers get to know you, and you learn the history of the house and its rules and customs. This was really the first time I felt like I belonged in a group. I had played football and volleyball in high school, but this was a new type of organization to be a part of. The other guys that rushed with me would become some of the most genuine friends I would have outside of the military.

I met my best friend during rush. Sean P. Keeley was a six two, slender Irishman who always wore blue jeans and a white T-shirt. He was two years older than me, very energetic, and a comedian. He told wonderful stories from his childhood and experiences from growing up in Michigan.

There were many ups and downs that came with school and the fraternity. I got to explore about myself and to learn how to listen to drunks and their exploits. The alumni were amazing. They had money for booze, told stories about their past, and spoke about their current jobs—I loved hearing all of it. They brought me a perspective of growing up and having a life after school. Hearing about their exciting lives after college made me realize that maybe I could do it, too.

Attending college offered me opportunities to meet new people and have new experiences that helped me grow as a man, and to learn how to go to class and study, to take care of your car, and to behave. It was not common for students to enlist in the army while in college. Most college kids would attend the cadet program at the college to become officers rather than joining the reserves as enlisted soldiers.

I faced several serious emotional blows while at Purdue. The loss of a child, the death of my best friend, and my first deployment to Afghanistan became new depths of hell that I was not equipped to handle. I dealt with these huge emotional challenges in the same way I had in high school—I didn't. I just tried to kill them with alcohol.

The college environment was great for a person who needed a place to hide in plain sight. Purdue provided a place where people could escape either through books or at the bar. Both were acceptable. For me, it was the booze.

I always felt like I learned more about life while at the bar than I did in the classroom or while studying. People shared their lives with me, and I listened to their lessons and stories. People seem more honest and open after a few drinks. I would also share more of my past, and I felt less angry at myself.

The college environment made it easy to fall in line with drinking and being a part of something felt really good. I was a good drinker, and I had plenty of friends who also loved to drink. I'm sure I spent well over $10,000 on alcohol while in college for just over four years. It worked to manage my pain, but it's not a healthy way to cope with the pain and problems of the past. Drinking caused lots of new problems. I had to make up my own rules to follow about my drinking. I would stay on campus to finish all my assignments prior to going home because I knew that if I started drinking, I wouldn't stop, and no schoolwork would get done.

While at Purdue, I received two charges of underage drinking and picked up a charge of public intoxication on a different night. The alcohol started to tear apart my stomach. I vomited a lot. Alcohol tore apart my pocketbook too, and eventually, it would tear apart my mind.

As the years went on, I would only drink on Fridays, Saturdays, and during holidays. Binge-drinking on the weekends was the norm. I was making up for lost time, getting rid of the built-up stress that the work week had caused. Drinking alcohol is generally accepted everywhere. I think it's the most destructive drug to the human body; it can be bought over the counter in almost any store in America. Alcohol was easy to find, and it was cheap. So, it was a perfect way for me to soothe my pain.

———

While I rushed Theta Xi fraternity, my stepfather's sentencing took place. I told my soon-to-be fraternity brothers that I would have to miss some of the initiation process. The group of us was on the dance floor, which was on the second floor of the house. We all were standing in a circle, locking arms, when I told them about what had happened to me. I explained that I had been sexually abused as a kid and that I was going to put the man who did this to me in jail. They hugged me and offered me kind words about how brave I was. Instead of shunning me and making me feel bad about my past, my new friends showed me support throughout the process. My friends were open to listening to the stories of my childhood, and I never felt as if I was an outsider amongst the group. I felt accepted.

Telling them was a big risk. If they had reacted a different way, I might not have been able to be so open with others in the future. I've never really been harmed by telling the truth. This was a time in which I became more comfortable talking about my past and stopped caring about what others thought about what had happened to me. That dance floor in the fraternity was pivotal in allowing me to be open and honest with who I am to others as opposed to being a recluse.

I had prepared for my day in court for years. I wore my best suit. The suit hung off my body weirdly, and I felt uncomfortable because my mom made me wear a tie. At the sentencing, I made the choice to share some of the stories of abuse with the judge and the courtroom. Speaking about the past was the hardest thing I had ever been asked to do. I had to explain how I was touched, how his penis touched me, how I was ejaculated on, and how my stepfather took advantage of my body and my innocence.

While I was on the stand, I was all alone; none of my family was able to be in the courtroom. It was divided into two sections with wooden rows of seats like pews in a church. His family sat on the far side, away from me. After I described the abuse to the judge and was cross-examined, my stepfather's mother stood up in the courtroom and yelled, "He's a fucking liar!" This outburst was very shocking to me, especially since my stepfather had confessed to the sexual abuse he'd done to me. The judge asked her to sit, and said if she had another outburst, she would be removed from the courtroom.

My stepfather was sentenced to spend eight years in prison.

———

There was still one detail about the abuse that took another twenty years for me to understand and put into words. I had many confusing thoughts about my sexuality. I liked to be touched, but this is what tortured me. I could never turn off these types of thoughts. They were repeated every day and every year. Over the years of sexual abuse, I learned that being touched felt very good. This filled me with confusion and shame.

I have thought about the whys and hows of the sexual abuse I endured for a very long time. My stepfather stated that he himself was sexually abused when he was young. I don't understand why someone would continue to commit the same actions that also hurt them at a younger age. Another answer I received as to why someone thought these abuses happened to me is because I am a very loving person and show a lot of emotion. Someone mentioned that I am empathetic and that this was a likeable trait that my stepfather enjoyed about me.

These answers just don't make sense to me, but they are the best answers I received and the best answers I will likely ever get. My mother didn't have many answers for me either, nor could she explain why she didn't notice what was happening to me earlier than she did.

———

There were many other significant events that happened while I was at Purdue that I will carry with me until I die. The loss of my best friend, Sean P. Keeley, was one of them. Sean hung himself on or around April 5, 2002. The loss of Kayla Hurst, an ex-girlfriend who was murdered, along with two of her friends, at Ohio State University on July 22, 2003, was another. In addition, a young woman I was dating named L.J. got pregnant. Her mother said the family would cut her off if she went through with the pregnancy. She was forced by her parents to have an abortion. Some years later, her mother would commit suicide.

It wasn't just the abuses I'd endured as a child. As more and more traumas continued to pile up, new scenes were added that would replay in my mind like a horror film. These scenes compounded in my brain.

Eventually, I would learn a lot more about brain health. I came to understand that these traumatic events were actually injuries rather than some kind of disorder. Unfortunately, while I was a university student, this understanding was still a long way off.

———

In the year 2000, when I was nineteen, I found a painful lump on my breast. I reached out to my mother to tell her what was happening and how the lump felt large and round. My mother is the best person in my life to ask questions about what might be growing inside me. After my mother felt the mass in my left breast, she recommended that I get it removed and examined to see if it was cancerous. My mother was very clinical about my care. It felt like I was her patient rather than her son.

A few years earlier, my mother had had a full hysterectomy to remove a softball-sized mass that had grown inside her. Hers was not cancerous, but it was scary to see her go through the surgery and the pain of recovery. During my mom's recovery, she was very self-sufficient and was able to take care of herself. I would have surgery on my breast to remove the mass. I had a lot of strong feelings during the time when the mass was being tested. It was scary to think that I might have to go through cancer treatment and that my life could change dramatically. A biopsy was performed on the mass, and it was found to be benign.

In December 2000, at the age of twenty, I decided to join the army. One of the greatest things I thought the army could provide me with was a chance to have an honorable death, potentially in battle, rather than by suicide. I was also running away from my life. To that point, I had not made much of myself. I think I was trying to prove to myself that I could be a soldier. I just wanted to have the skill to fight if the United States ever needed me to fight in a war.

After I had enlisted in the Army Reserves, my mother wanted us to go on a trip together. I think she wanted us to spend some time together before I was to ship off to Fort Jackson, South Carolina for basic training in April 2021.

Drew Brees and Purdue had just won the Big Ten and were slated to play in the Rose Bowl on January 1, 2001. So, my mom and I decided to head west and made a road trip out of it.

My mom planned our route from Indiana to Texas and New Mexico, through Arizona, and on into California. On our return, we would drive to the Four Corners in Las Vegas; this location marks the point at which the borders of four different U.S. states meet: Utah, Arizona, Colorado and New Mexico. Then, we would cut through Colorado on the way back to Indiana. Our first stop was Odessa, Texas, where we spent some time with family members. I was told that I had visited Odessa when I was young, but I couldn't remember it. My family in Odessa raised horses and barrel raced, and it felt nice to be around horses again.

After Odessa, we visited Window Rock, Arizona, where my cousin worked as a physical therapist on a Navajo Reservation. The conditions on the Navajo reservation made me think they were living in a third-world country. The homes looked worn down, and the people didn't have access to running water. I felt sad and didn't understand why Americans would allow people to live this way. Window Rock is an outstanding rock formation that has been shaped by the wind. It was a sight to see. The dark red colors and the veins of the rock formation ran all around the stone; it was worth the hike to get a closer look.

After Window Rock, we traveled to Flagstaff and took a northern route into the Grand Canyon. My mom and I got a campsite near the South Rim. I have a few pictures from the Grand Canyon while I was near the edge of a cliff. I spent some time there thinking about my past while soaking up the vastness of the Canyon. It made me feel small, but my thoughts were just as enormous as what I was seeing. I thought about how this place would have felt like as a settler, seeing it for the first time.

My mom and I made it back to our campsite to make a fire and pitch our tent. The fire gave my mom and me a chance to talk; she said she was really proud of me for joining the army. My decision to join made her believe that I would become something more than just sad and depressed. I think the army might have been a symbol to show her that I had gotten better. Of course, I hadn't gotten better; I just lied about how I felt. I had learned how to use my words a bit better than I had in the past to explain my life to her. I remember it being very cold, and I ended up sleeping in the car all night.

In California, I was dropped off at a fraternity brother's apartment in Redondo Beach, with the intent to meet up with my mother later. It was an incredible place that felt so fresh and alive. We played football on the beach together and spotted dolphins diving in the waves. The dolphins moved effortlessly through the water. It was fascinating to watch them move in precise synchronization. I was surrounded by water, and I felt peaceful and calm for the first time in many years. The sand on my feet allowed me to feel grounded.

The only bummer was that I was only twenty and didn't have an ID to get into the clubs. We tried to get into a club in downtown LA on New Year's Eve, but I was turned away. I got a ride through Beverly Hills and was starstruck by how large the houses were. All the homes were huge, painted white, with massive front lawns and multiple cars—a view I didn't know existed. This was totally different from Chicago and West Lafayette.

I met up with some other Theta Xi members from the Purdue chapter at the Theta Xi house at UCLA. The house was phenomenal, and the architecture reminded me of a castle from medieval times, a place that I had only read about in history books. The house even had a zip line where people would zip down and land in the pool in the backyard.

The next day, all the Purdue fraternity brothers went to

the Rose Bowl and watched Purdue lose. I had no way to get ahold of my mom. The plan was to meet each other after the game so that we could drive to Las Vegas together. Simply by luck, my mom found me in the parking lot in Pasadena—I think it was a bit of a miracle. We then drove to Vegas, where we went to see a Cirque du Soleil show at Treasure Island. The show was an absolutely mind-bending display of human strength and flexibility. I liked Vegas so much that I would go back there for my mid-tour leave during my first trip to Afghanistan.

From Las Vegas, we traveled to Aspen, Colorado, which was another marvelous place because of the mountains and snow. Getting into Denver from there was a truly breath-taking drive. After Denver, the land was flat and very bland. My mother spent this last part of our trip sleeping and arguing with me while smoking cigarettes. I drove from Denver to Indianapolis, the longest I had ever spent behind the wheel. The drive took us around twenty hours.

Driving through much of the United States had a large impact on me. I enjoyed seeing the places that I had only heard of or seen in movies and magazines. Visiting the various natural rock formations, several Native American history museums, and Indigenous people's homes was intriguing for me. This trip allowed me to get a perspective of the people who lived here before the Europeans arrived and helped me understand that the land had been stolen from the Native Americans. I felt the desire to help people who were oppressed and seemingly forgotten in history.

I headed back to Purdue with many new perspectives while preparing for basic training. The world was so vast. Exploring America gave me a better respect for the United

States and all the people living in different ways. This trip helped to expand my thinking and parts of the United States I had no idea existed. I knew that I would be going to basic training in April 2001, so I did not enroll in the spring semester at Purdue. I was sent to Fort Jackson, South Carolina.

The type of structure the army provided made sense to me, and it was what I needed at that confusing time in my life. The army takes people's choices away. I didn't have to worry about when I ate or what clothes I had to wear. Everyone was treated by the same standard; I knew what was expected of me and what duties I needed to perform. It was an amazing experience, but the reason I joined the army was not to serve the nation.

Being in the army provided me with many new skills such as caring for my feet, clearing weapons, taking long road marches, performing drill and ceremony, and generally learning to be a soldier. A very important skill was the ability to take another human being's life. At basic training, I had to focus my mind and body on learning how to kill strangers. Going through the Special Forces qualification course, I developed the skills of planning, training, and being technically proficient in the manners of unconventional warfare. The main focus was taking the lives of humans. After twenty-five weeks of basic training followed by advanced training, I returned to Purdue and resumed my life at Theta Xi. I had more pride in myself and way more discipline.

At Theta Xi, like in the army, being surrounded by a group of people who enjoyed living and being together was powerful to me. This community and sense of belonging felt bigger than myself.

I usually went to Purdue football games with all the members of the fraternity on Saturday mornings. Game day has more meaning when you're twenty-one. Being in the stands with my brothers felt like family. I lived for game day, booze, parties, and women. It was a shared experience, and it felt as if we were one. There was a very important shared time that wasn't any fun at all, when we lost one of our own, Sean P. Keeley, to suicide.

Sean's death made me feel like I had lost a real brother. I kept telling myself I could've done more to change his actions, but I understood how he felt inside. His suicide made me become very distant and took my mind to a dark place. No one could ever really tell what I had going on inside because I had learned early in life how to keep things compartmentalized and quiet. I cried, drank, did drugs, listened to music, and cried some more.

The other side of this enormous grief was the fact that, for the first time, I actually had people around me who were feeling the same loss. We would all talk with each other about losing Sean. We came together as a brotherhood and shared the pain together. I created internal emotions by drinking heavily. I would black out but believe that people could not recognize that I was extremely intoxicated. I have always gone to extremes in everything in my life. It's just who I am, and I have to be careful.

The house on campus was surrounded by tall oak trees, and there was a shortcut path leading to another part of the property. The leaves would turn a wonderful orange-yellow color in the fall which looked like a brilliant sunset. The leaves would fall all around the house and stay there for quite a while because raking and bagging leaves was probably the last thing on a college kid's mind. The leaves would get wet with the snow and rain which would create a mess everywhere.

On one particular day, I can't remember exactly which aspect of my life made me feel sad, but it drew me to the small forest behind our fraternity house. I think I had had a serious talk about breaking up with a girl—I'm not completely sure. I found myself sitting on the ground, leaning against a tree, looking up at the sky, watching the leaves fall from the treetops. It seemed as if the leaves were a shower all around me. It took my breath away to see the sun filter the colors through the leaves and onto my eyes. I picked one up. With my eyes tearing up, I thought that even though these leaves had lost their source of life, they were still beautiful. They were dying, but they were still able to bring me happiness.

An idea formed within me—*hat you could still have a purpose and meaning even after you have lost your source of life*. The moment with the leaves helped me through a long period of pain and depression. What the trees and leaves stood for had so much more meaning to me. Something beautiful was captured in my heart.

I took a single leaf, put it in a frame, and kept it on my desk. If anyone asked me why I had a framed leaf on my desk, I shared my thoughts about how the leaves had made me feel and how they represented hope when it was hard to find hope inside me. After I had told this story many times, I decided it was time to end the on-again, off-again relationship with my then-girlfriend.

Some days afterward, I returned to my room and noticed that my leaf had been ripped into several pieces and put back into the frame. *What the fuck? How could a person do this to something that brought me so much joy and had so much meaning?* My ex-girlfriend had done this to get back at me because she was so upset that I didn't want to have a relationship with her. I kept the torn-up leaves in the frame for a few more years.

The scariest letter I have ever opened arrived in January 2003. It was from the Indiana Army Reserves, stating that I needed to prepare to deploy to Iraq.

In the months leading up to that summer, I prepared to deploy with my unit. I left Purdue before the semester ended but received partial credit for my work. I spent three months in Georgia, at Fort Stewart and Fort Gordon. I was twenty-two years old; patriotic duty was at an all-time high. America had begun invading Iraq, and it seemed as if all citizens stood united as one. Near the end of my mobilization, which had prepared me to deploy to Iraq, I started to feel that my military occupation as a hospital food service tech would not be needed in the hospital in Iraq. The casualties were not going to hospitals; they were being flown to Germany. My job had no purpose, so I was sent back home to Indiana.

I returned to Purdue and restarted school. In the fall, I transferred from the Indiana Reserves to the Indiana National Guard. I met a recruiter who mentioned that, based on my assessments, I was more suited to be a part of a combat-focused unit; I also felt that I would to fit in better here.

I joined the 151st Long-Range Surveillance Detachment (LRSD) because I felt that I would be surrounded by more like-minded warriors. I joined the unit as a cook, as that was the only position that was available. Our unit prepared to mobilize for a year-long deployment to Afghanistan.

When I was mobilized to Afghanistan in 2004, I had to

attend infantry training camp at Camp Robinson, Arkansas. While I was at the training, I slept next to a young soldier in the barracks, Specialist / E-4 (SPC) Norman Snyder, age nineteen. While SPC Snyder went through training, I observed things that made me think that he should not be deploying to Afghanistan. I told him, "If you go to Afghanistan, you are going to die." These words still haunt me today.

After training, we headed to Manas Air Force Base in Kyrgyzstan. We weren't there long before we flew into Bagram Air Force Base, about an hour outside of Kabul in Afghanistan, then on to Camp Phoenix on the north side of Kabul. I was then stationed in Kandahar Airfield (KAF), east of Kandahar city; my unit began going on pay missions to Camp Price and other distant firebases around Kandahar province for the Afghan National Army.

Camp Price is named after Chief Bruce E. Price, a Green Beret who was killed while on patrol in the town of Kajaki, which is about sixty miles northwest of Kandahar. Chief Price was a member of the 1st Battalion of the 3rd Special Forces group. This is the same group I would eventually be assigned to in November 2009.

Camp Price was north of Lashkar Gah in the south of Afghanistan, but west of Kandahar City. We drove light-skinned trucks with little to no armor. I carried a machine gun and mounted the gun on top of the trucks. I generally took a position where I was standing up out of the center of the truck. Our team of ten traveled on Route One to get to the firebase. This route would become very dangerous, and my Operational Detachment Alpha (ODA) almost lost a few teammates due to an improvised explosive device (IED). However, at that time, these pay missions were something that gave my unit more of a purpose than just being the security element at Camp Phoenix in Kabul.

Someone that gave us something to look forward to that year was the comedian and actor, Robin Williams. As I listened to Robin Williams in 2004 at Kandahar Airfield, Afghanistan, he made me laugh and feel at home. Williams spoke across Camp Brown, the Special Forces compound, while I stood in the volleyball courts that were in front of the old military exchange (PX) near the terminal airfield. The stage lit up just this portion of the camp; everything else was pitch black.

As Robin spoke, dust filled the sky, and the spinning of helicopter blades could be heard in the distance. Every few minutes, a rumble would start at my boots then zoom through my whole body. I glanced over my shoulder to see a ten-foot flame streaming out of the jet. The noise from the jet shook my eyes. I smelled feces wafting through my nose every few minutes, mixed with burning trash and tires. This smell sits in your nose until you can get a clean shower. All the noise became a sound machine, a background noise that you don't notice. *This is war,* I thought.

I have always been grateful that Mr. Williams took some of his time spending it with the troops doing a comedy routine. I was twenty-four, and it made me feel that America cared about us in a faraway land.

———

Every day in Afghanistan could have been my last, but I did have another significant health scare. One evening, I felt a BB-sized lump in one of my testicles. I went to the doctor to seek further care. I was directed to Bagram Air Force Base for an ultrasound of my testicles. I was able to get to Bagram a few weeks later when we had a convoy going there from Camp Phoenix in Kabul.

The male doctor told me to lie down on my back and pull my pants down so he could examine me. It felt weird to have another man touch me again. It certainly brought back a lot of memories of my younger years, but I made the choice for my health, and myself, to be vulnerable enough so that I could find out if I had cancer in my body. After the examination, the doctor informed me that the mass was a normal thing that can happen in and around the testicles—nothing unusual. But my thoughts of dying in Afghanistan were still there and present every day.

I remember the tower at Camp Price. It was 100 feet in the air, and there was an MK-19 bolted to the top. The MK-19 (pronounced Mark 19) is an American 40 mm belt-fed automatic grenade launcher. The trucks that the ODA had were loaded to fight and had guns attached to all sides of them.

The firebase was surrounded by barriers that provided some sense of security. While we were there, we had access to the team house and were able to relax on their couches and watch TV. I had a small DVD player to watch movies on, and other guys had personal laptops. To actually have a living room set-up made me feel like I was at home. The ODA members were very welcoming to us. It just felt more like home than living in green army tents.

Most ODA members had beards, which was something I knew I would not be able to achieve since I pretty much didn't have any hair on my body. I felt that this was the group of humans I wanted to be a part of if I was going to continue my military career.

On my return ride home from Afghanistan, I thought about Camp Price and my experiences with the Special Forces members. I knew I was going to finish my bachelor's degree in history at Purdue, but I would now elect to focus on classes that dealt with the Middle East so that I could have a better understanding of the history and culture of the part of the world I was working in. I wanted to understand how and why the people in the Middle East live the way they do, the way they treat each other, the call to prayer, and the way they prepare different foods. I had made my decision that I was going to become a Special Forces soldier, and I was going to prepare myself for the future.

Before I left Afghanistan, on March 26, 2005, Norman Snyder was killed when he drove his non-tactical vehicle over a land mine, killing himself and three others, just four months before he was supposed to return home. I had to carry their remains to the helicopter at Camp Phoenix.

———

I've heard many people say something to the effect of, "You can't understand war unless you have been in it." I believe this statement to be false. I think that the language a person uses must describe their experiences, and people need to be shown how to express themselves clearly. People need their stories to "paint the picture" so others can picture it in their minds. The depiction of the environment is easy; that's the "where." The *feelings* of that place can be the most difficult part to describe. I have noticed that war veterans often skip the explaining phase of war because it is just *understood,* the loneliness, the feeling that you could die at any moment, the bright stars at night when you are in a place that doesn't have streetlights or a city glow. Yes, war is hell and remarkably difficult to understand, let alone explain to people who have never been in it. But the feelings of war can be very different from what most humans go through in their lives. I like to say, "Explain it like Disney World."

I remember going to Disney World as a kid. This was a magical place that was far away from anything I'd ever seen in Indiana. Epcot Center had different types of buildings and foods I'd never experienced. When I returned home, I was able to talk with my friends about how the Disney World experience felt, smelled, and looked. I have taken this Disney World model with me along my trauma journey, and I've used it to explain to people about war or other difficult subjects. People just need to practice speaking the words, and then do some more practice in developing their skills to share their thoughts and what they have been through.

Holding onto trauma will never help you get better. Trauma needs many hours of conversation and contemplation. Explaining what you have done and seen shouldn't be something you are afraid of doing. You grow from telling your story.

———

My mother's father was in WWII as an infantry soldier in the US Army and was wounded twice during his time in Europe. He used to take me and my brother fishing when we were kids. He was a simple, Hungarian man who worked his ass off for everything he had. He owned a fruit and vegetable stand for a time. I also remember him driving an 18-wheeler for Alka-Seltzer, Bayer, and Goodyear tires. He enjoyed being on the road and exploring the United States as well as watching NBA basketball. Grandpa died in 1996 before I joined the

Army. I was sixteen when he passed. I think he would've shared more of the experiences he'd had during the war if I had been deployed prior to his passing away.

I will refer to what is commonly known as PTSD as PTSI, or post-traumatic stress injury, because it really is an injury, not a disorder, and it is directly linked to the military. I think when people hear or talk about PTSI, they assume it is trauma you get from active duty either in Iraq or Afghanistan. Trauma affects everyone. Every. Single. Human. Being. I think about PTSI as the hazard of living a human being's life. There will be stresses and tough situations that every human being will go through while they experience living.

H&S 220K - Death Dying Human Health, was one of the last classes I took during my last semester at Purdue. By that August, I knew I was going to try and go on active duty and attempt to join the Special Forces Green Berets. I thought this class would help prepare me for my future life in the army. I wanted to learn about dealing with the potential loss of my teammates.

This class was far from what I was expecting. We learned about how different cultures deal with dying. The class presented the stages of grief and how people from around the world viewed death in their families and cultures. It was one of the worst classes I took over the years at Purdue. The student teacher was awful. He wanted to grade assignments as if he were an English professor. I didn't realize I was taking a class where misspellings on exams made answers incorrect. The greatest thing I was able to get out of the course was that the love of my life was in the same class.

I spent a semester arguing about life and death with this girl. She stood five feet and five inches tall, with silk brown dark hair and bright blue eyes. I remember the first time I saw her walk into the classroom. She wore a red Chi Omega rain jacket, representing the sorority that she belonged to. The Chi Omega house was where all the hot girls rushed at Purdue. I thought to myself, *Please let me get to know her.* Her name was Shawn—yes, the same name as my brother. At first, we didn't seem like much of a match, but there was definitely some type of connection.

On December 16, 2006, the night before I was to graduate from Purdue, I was celebrating at Harry's Chocolate Shop, a favorite local bar. This is where I spent most of my drinking years at Purdue. Harry's Chocolate Shop has a rich history all the way back to before the prohibition era. Their slogan is, "Go ugly early."

I sure as hell went ugly that night. I had been drinking for several hours before I saw Shawn walk through the bar. I met her on the back side of the bar near the stairs to the second floor. As we were talking, I started to feel sick to my stomach. I found the nearest trash can and puked right in it. Shawn got me some water, which I used to wash the puke out of my mouth. Then, I reached for her and pulled her in close to me for a kiss. She was sober, and I was drunk, but she didn't resist even though she had just watched me throw up. It was love at first puke! From that first night at Harry's, we've been together ever since.

In the beginning, a lot of our relationship was long-distance. We learned that many of our values aligned. We were very compatible. Through some tough conversations, we learned where we really stood with each other. While Shawn finished school at Purdue, I spent a lot of time at Fort Benning and Fort Bragg. I began training to become a Green

Beret during my last semester at Purdue. I started walking around with this awful ruck, or "tick," for countless hours and miles. I walked around Purdue with a ruck on my back like the one Forrest Gump wore when he ran with soldiers. I would spend hours in the gym lifting weights and riding a stationary bike.

I was training for the future, for selection. It was my goal to become a Green Beret, and there was nothing that was going to stop me from being successful. I knew I could prepare my body. All I needed was some time. So, I chose to spend my time walking, running, and lifting to become the most physically fit that I could. The psychological aspect of becoming a Green Beret was not a concern to me. I knew that I could mentally suffer more than anyone. There was no amount of food or sleep deprivation that could make me quit. My bigger concern was about my body failing me.

MILITARY

The Trauma Continues

In April 2007, after only a few months of Shawn and I getting to know each other, I left for active duty. A few months after that, I arrived at Fort Bragg. I lived in an old barracks near the wind tunnel on Gruber Road until I passed the Special Forces Assessment and Selection (SFAS) and was selected. The barracks was an animal house of sorts. They housed guys who were young and who were preparing to go to selection. There was a lot of drinking and fighting, but not in a bad manner. It felt like my second fraternity house. The lecture hall at Purdue was nothing like my new lecture hall, Camp Mackall.

Camp Mackall, North Carolina, is about forty miles to the west of Fort Bragg and it's where Green Berets are either made or destroyed. It's black and white. At least, that's how the cadre, the instructors that are running the course, made it feel to me. I went to Camp Mackall in June to attend the Special Operations Prep Course (SOPC). This was the course an eighteen-x-ray would attend prior to selection. An eighteen-x-ray enlistment will allow a person to go straight to the SFAS after completing basic training and airborne school, rather than attempting to attend SFAS after the person gets to their final duty station. SOPC consisted of physical training, map reading, land navigation, and the Nasty Nick obstacle course which has at least fifteen obstacles. There are ropes to climb that reach heights of twenty-five feet in the air, monkey bars, and underground tunnels. This prep course is where I made many of the friends I would have during the rest of the qualification course to become a Green Beret.

SOPC was awful. We slept, ate, and did physical fitness. Also, it was the hottest environment I had ever experienced in my life. My class would basically get smoked all day; the cadre would put us through physical drills of push-ups, sit-ups, and crawling on the ground. But the best thing that came out of SOPC was that we became familiar with the training area of Camp Mackall. Similar to *Forrest Gump* again, we would run... everywhere! This knowledge of the camp helped to decrease my anxiety about the "ultimate" test of going to Special Forces Assessment and Selection (SFAS). I knew my surroundings, and this would become a great advantage during team week and Small Unit Tactics.

Due to all the work I put in during my last semester at Purdue, I felt as if I was prepared for SOPC. The prep course increased my speed, rucking, and running skills. It truly was just preparation for the next phase, the brutal test to determine whether I could become a Green Beret.

Selection was completely different from what I had pictured. I thought there would be more interaction with the cadre, but all the instructions we needed were just written on a whiteboard. You had to be at the right place at the right time with the right equipment. The board would say something like, "One gallon of water with a jug, a pair of running shoes, black socks, army T-shirt, and army shorts at 5:00 am." I started SFAS at Pike Field on Fort Bragg in the old WWII barracks. The barracks were very run-down buildings with shitty living conditions, but no one cared. I was focused on performing well. I crushed the army physical fitness test, which was two minutes of push-ups and two minutes of sit-ups and completed as many repetitions as possible in the time limit. We normally just ran a two-mile run, but at SFAS, all of us had to run a five-mile. This was the fastest five miles I have ever run. I was twenty-six years old and in the best shape of my life.

We were transported out to Camp Mackall in cattle trucks. The trips to Camp Mackall for each new phase or new course began to feel the same. There would be time for introspection, and I would constantly have thoughts that I was going to crush whatever was presented to me—I would never quit. At SFAS, when I was told to run, I ran fast. When I was told to walk, I walked and waited until some cadre would tell me to stop. I never ran with a ruck on my back, even though everyone around me took off at a dead sprint. I walked at the same pace throughout the whole selection. I knew that if I tried to run, it would increase my chances of blisters and getting injured.

During team week, I helped my teammates by lifting heavy telephone poles, huge ammunition steel boxes, and sandbags for long periods of time. I just didn't care about the additional work. More miles? More weight? Yes, please! I had the best selection team that could have ever been put together.

The main thing I needed at this time was one of my favorite things in the world: WATER! It was so fucking hot in North Carolina in August, at least ninety-nine degrees with 100 percent humidity. SFAS ran a reverse cycle due to the extreme heat. We did pretty much everything at night because of the risk of heat injuries. I didn't have any issues with this change in schedule. I took great care of my feet by cleaning them with rubbing alcohol, sleeping without socks, then wearing clean socks every day. I always took a shower before I went to sleep.

Taking care of my body was the priority. There wasn't much mental stress or complex thinking during SFAS. Selection evaluates your physical strengths, and the outcome of what stress does to your leadership skills. The training actually gave me time to focus more on the trauma I'd endured as a child and my thoughts on trauma overall.

From my perspective, trauma has a way of heightening the true person inside each of us. If you are an outgoing person, or a lazy, self-centered person, then trauma makes those characteristics more noticeable. If you are always thinking, *Poor me* and *It's all my fault*, then I think you're more likely to use your trauma as an excuse for when life gets hard. Being a human is hard; now add other humans. I think you either live with trauma and become it—identify as that trauma—or you can take that trauma and use it as fuel to make you a better person. Yes, it is difficult, and yes, there have been months and years that I didn't remember where my trauma could be a benefit, too, and I played the victim. When playing the victim, I spent a lot of time thinking about how I could change those situations.

My trauma gave me a continually active mind that I used for a lot of introspection about life and other human beings. Throughout Green Beret selection, there were many times when I was alone walking through the woods and down the roads in and around Camp Mackall. Often, I would dream about how my life would have been if I had never been abused. The trauma I endured would replay in my mind. Many times, I felt frustrated and angry, but I never took much time to focus on my emotions while also feeling hot, cold, wet, hungry, or tired. My trauma was a tool for my success. I would say to myself, *I know how this could be worse— I could be back in that trailer.* I just didn't care about the pain. In a way, I lived for the pain. The pain made me *feel.*

I was walking with my past, mile by mile. Thoughts about

a better future kept me busy. Being at Camp Mackall and on my future trips to Afghanistan gave me the freest feelings I'd experienced. Seeing the world through fresh eyes at Camp Mackall and later in Afghanistan showed me how it truly felt to be alive. There wasn't as much noise of the world in those places. Many times, it was just me and the *boys*.

September 2, 2007, was a special day. I stood in a formation of 380 men who had completed the twenty-one days of selection. Slowly, the numbers were called off and the group was separated into two. As I heard the roster numbers being called off, I noticed that the numbers were those of the lowest performers. I began to get nervous about hearing my roster number. My roster number was seven. When the cadre sounded off with a slow seventy-seven, for a split second, I thought that I had failed. The number seven never got called out. There were only seventy-five of us standing when all the numbers had been called. There was no order or sequence, it was random numbers. This kept us on edge, which felt like an eternity. I was selected to continue to the Q-course, and I would start the path of earning my Green Beret. It was my twenty-seventh birthday.

———

Shawn and I did our best to see each other as much as we could during selection and beyond. We would spend our time together doing lovebird-type things. We would drink together and spend time at bars. We tended to get late-night Taco Bell, or calzones, or cheese sticks. We would sleep in and waste our mornings together. There were very few concerns or stressful things in our lives during the early years. It was the perfect time to develop a lasting love for each other.

Shawn fell in love with me because I made her feel protected. She'll also say that it was because I was as good-looking as a Calvin Klein model and that I'm the funniest person she knows. These things are part of the inside banter that we still have to this day.

Shawn is an incredibly strong-willed individual. I knew that she would be able to hold her own on her own if anything ever happened to me. She has a fire to learn and is continuously developing herself. She had a desire for a higher education, which was important to me. Our relationship grew deeper, and we could see how formidable we would be as a team.

I was initially against having children because of what happened to me in my younger life. Shawn and I would really talk about how she thought I would make an exceptional father, and about how she felt I would be a great protector of her and any future children we might have. Once again, someone else had to believe in me before I could believe in myself. She saw I could be a great father when I didn't see it myself.

These conversations would give me lots to think about as I was back and forth between Shawn and the Special Forces qualification course. For me, there were eight phases or courses that you attended during the qualification course. When phases would end, we generally got time off to return home. I always made it back to Indiana to see her.

I wrote letters and sent flowers to Shawn on a weekly basis. The courses within the Q-course were at all different lengths. Sometimes, I wouldn't talk with Shawn for about a month, maybe more. I was focused on getting through the Q-course while she was focused on studying and graduating from Purdue. Shawn wanted to become a behaviorist, a study which focuses on applied behavioral analysis, with the goal of becoming a Board Certified Behavior Analyst. We did our best to talk as often as possible and see each other when we could. I would surprise her by showing up at Purdue when there were course breaks or during holiday weekends.

My first major course, Small Unit Tactics (SUT), was an introduction to ODA-style tactical movements and strategy, which could be evaluated by instructors or the cadre. The course evaluated your leadership style when you were tired, hungry, and uncomfortable. You had to care about your team, the equipment, and your weapons. We had to move through Pineland as a team to accomplish the missions we were assigned. Pineland, the land that surrounds Camp Mackall, is just the land that we trained on. Green berets are made here. Pineland has grown and broken some of the hardest men that I know.

The cadre evaluated the team, and then we swapped leadership roles to complete more missions. The team I was on performed very well for that phase. The cadre really wanted us to learn leadership and decision making in rough physical and mental states.

Language school was absolutely the worst portion of the Q-course for me. I struggled in school as a child, and in college, and this course was no different. Learning French was the hardest thing for me to internalize. I would end up being *recycled* twice for failing the defense language proficiency test. So, I spent ten months in a French class which should have only taken me four months to complete. My mind had a really challenging time with grammar rules, and the memorization of vocabulary just didn't stick easily for me.

I drove to Purdue after failing my French language course the first time. I needed a break. I had completed four months of forty-hour weeks just to fail. I was angry with myself because I knew I had given everything that I had to learn and study French. I just had a really challenging time learning this information. I have never been assessed for ADHD or received an official diagnosis of a learning disability.

In December 2008, I was going to propose to Shawn. I had made a down payment and saved money to purchase the ring. The ring was the biggest purchase that I had made for another person. And the choice, to ask the girl I loved to marry me, was the biggest decision I had ever made.

It was Christmas, and the time to ask Shawn to marry me had arrived. We were staying at her parents' home in Lafayette, a two-story, simple-looking house with a front and back yard and a two-car garage full of Shawn's father's knick-knacks like old baseball caps, empty beer cans, and Purdue memorabilia that Shawn's mother insisted stay outside of the house.

Inside there was a fireplace with a welcoming fire burning. A small hint of burning wood was always in the air with a soft ground coffee scent mixed in. It was a typical American home with four bedrooms and two-and-a-half baths. The gathering place around the television consisted of three couches and a glass coffee table. It felt like home. I brought the ring with me since I knew I was going to ask her parents if I could have Shawn's hand in marriage. Shawn's parents were sitting in the living room watching the fire. I kept on walking around the house, from the front door through the kitchen to the living room and back. I was sliding around on their hardwood floor with my socks. I was just so nervous to bring up the conversation, and her parents could tell something was up.

I finally grabbed the ring out of my winter jacket and sat down with Shawn's parents. They had one big question for me, "Why do you think our daughter is the right woman for you?" I told them that Shawn was the strongest and smartest woman that I had ever known. She had shown me that she would be able to take care of a family when I deployed. Shawn has an exceptional work ethic and had shown me that she cares for others along with herself. Plus, she has a better sense of humor than I do. Shawn would be able to survive if anything happened to me. She has the strength to carry all my stuff and manage her life, too. I had always known Shawn to be the right woman for me.

Dave and Judy listened to my answers and ended up giving me their blessing to marry their daughter. Before we would get married though, we both had courses to finish. Shawn had her program at Purdue, and I had to wrap up the Q-course.

There would be a shift from physical prowess to mental prowess throughout the Q-course, when Robin Sage would test my mind. The Robin Sage examination was the last phase of the course that I had to go through before earning the Green Beret. Robin Sage lasted about a month; the course is broken up into parts. The first two weeks were to prepare our equipment, develop a plan, and establish our lines of effort for the following two weeks. The next two weeks we spent in the woods conducting military exercises. I was super excited to head back to Camp Mackall because it had been so long since I had been out to the training area west of Fort Bragg. I had spent so much time in the French course and in Military Occupational Specialty (MOS) that I had lost the fear of going out to Camp Mackall. Throughout the entirety of the course, there is a fear of failing or getting hurt that was associated with Camp Mackall. Being in Robin Sage felt like being a senior in high school. You were at the top of the food chain. It was the baddest guys who stared down all the other candidates in SFAS and in SUT. Robin Sage was a show-down among peers. It felt really good to be at the top. Being good at it made me feel like I was supposed to be there. We had done every course up to that point, and we had just four more weeks to earn the coveted Green Beret.

The first two weeks, our team, which was made up of twelve men, was called Operational Detachment Alpha (ODA). We prepared for our mission brief and prepped our airdrop bundles for the exercise. It wasn't terribly difficult. As I was an eighteen echo (18E) Special Forces communicator, I would cut wires to certain lengths to make antennas and build a battery plan. The communication plan was simple and didn't take much time to build for the time I had to build it. I had to test my radios and make SATCOM communications by send-ing messages to the base station, and they would send mes-sages back to me on the other side of the camp.

The base station was the main place where each team would send their messages and then relay them to the cadre. The only bad thing about being an 18E is that it is the only testable MOS during Robin Sage. You had to perform and get the daily situation reports back to the base station. The situ-ation reports were the only way we could request air drops, update the higher headquarters (cadre) about how the field exercises were going, and report what we had been up to during the previous twenty-four hours.

My team would pack up all our gear into our rucks and another backpack that sat on top of our rucks. Altogether, these backpacks weighed about 110 pounds. We had to carry all our gear into the mountains. We were lucky we didn't have to complete an airborne operation and jump into Robin Sage. Instead, we landed in a small plane at a small airport in central North Carolina. I carefully carried all my gear off the plane, and we put all our equipment into a trailer. We lay in the bed of a pickup truck to make sure we weren't seen by the "enemy".

It felt ridiculous, but we tried our best to stay in the "role" and to react as if we were in a foreign country. We rode in the back of the truck for a few hours before we were told to get out and walk. We walked for twelve hours up and down the mountains before we finally made it to our resting point. We all fell asleep quickly, and no one pulled security that night.

We awoke to being told that we had to meet the guerrilla chief and gain access to the camp. We had to eat a worm as a rite of passage. It was silly—no big deal. We walked for another hour to get to the G-Base. There were tents that the role players had set up, and our cook had a huge fire going in the middle of the camp. My teammates and I slept in the same tent. Once we were set up in camp, the plan felt simple—either you were pulling security, or you were planning a mission.

We trained the role players on how to use different weapons when we went out on missions. I had a wonderful team, and we all worked well together. We never got blown out of our camp, and I got all the messages out to the cadre. I had done my job.

After about a week of living on MRE (Meals Ready-To-Eat), we had a mission to acquire a pig from a pig farm in town so that we could feed the men. This was a situation the cadre would put students into as a kind of rite of passage. Three of us went into the pig pen and tried to catch a pig. There was shit and slop everywhere. This pig was huge! The cadre just laughed and took pictures of us while we wrestled the 300-pound pig into submission.

Next, we had to carry the pig through the mountains while it screamed. I thought it was hilarious to hear the pig squeal. I am not sure why it made me laugh because I knew the pig was about to die, but it did.

We strung the pig up by its hind legs until it no longer touched the ground. The senior guy had a knife—with a surgical stick to the heart, the pig was dead. He then slit the pig's throat, and its blood rushed onto the ground. The belly of the pig was the second cut, and all its intestines fell into the hole. Any innards that remained were scooped out by hand. All the parts of the pig that we could not consume went into the hole and then were covered by the dirt that we had shoveled to the side of the hole. Everyone lived off pulled pork for the next seven days. I was on fire with the energy the pig provided. I could think and perform easily again. Hit after hit, our missions were successful.

The cadre came and told me that I couldn't send any more messages as the team's communicator and that I wasn't to lead any more missions either. I was complete at Robin Sage even though we had five more days until the exercise was officially over. The cadre had already validated that I could perform the skills necessary to graduate. The cadre needed to focus on assessing the other 18E on our team.

Next, I was captured on a recon of a factory, bound up and put in a chair. I had no idea if I was going to be rescued, or if I was going to be moved to Survival, Evasion, Resistance, Escape (SERE) camp, which is a simulated prison camp. Becoming a prisoner at this camp is always a fear that sits in the back of your mind when training in Pineland. Throughout the entirety of the course, the students would talk about their experiences. Being captured by the simulated enemy forces and sent to the SERE camp seemed to happen every once in a while.

In the distance, I heard a train coming and started to feel the ground beneath me shake. A train stopped outside of the building where I was being housed. The next minute, my teammates rescued me as they infiltrated the factory from the train! It was fucking awesome! We cleaned our gear, turned it in at Camp Mackall, and went back to Fort Bragg to complete the final phase of the qualification course—graduation. Graduation was a small ceremony where I got to don my green beret for the first time. It is a significant moment in every green beret's life that they will never forget.

———

Shawn graduated with a degree in behavioral neuroscience from Purdue in the spring of 2009 and ended up moving to Fort Bragg in June of that summer while I was still in the 18E MOS portion of the Q-course. Shawn was excited to move away from home and start living on her own. We lived in our friend's apartment in Fayetteville because he was deployed in Afghanistan and wanted someone to watch over his place while he was gone.

It was comforting to live with Shawn. A family was starting to form. Shawn took a job in nearby Cary, NC. I finished the Q-course in November. Shawn and I were married on December 19, 2009. Our wedding took place in Lafayette, with the reception at the Purdue Union. My father, mother, and brother attended the ceremony. Harry's Chocolate Shop hosted another glorious reception for us. It was great to see my fraternity brothers getting to know Shawn's sorority sisters better.

That day, I focused on Shawn. The one time I said that I wouldn't drink would be at our wedding. I kept my word. I didn't drink any alcohol during the wedding or the reception. Mother had told me that my father had gotten completely drunk at their wedding. I don't know if it was true, but the story impacted my decision not to drink at my wedding. We put our honeymoon on pause because I was about to deploy to Afghanistan again.

A whole twenty days after we got married, I found myself in Afghanistan on my second deployment at the Combined Joint Special Operations Task Force-Afghanistan (CJSOTF-A). I spent seven months as the Command Team Aide and Radio-telegraph Operator (RTO). Being a part of the command team allowed me to travel throughout Afghanistan and visit most of the teams that were scattered throughout the country.

Everywhere I went, these special operators were surviving on the bare minimum of life's needs, namely, food, water, and safety. Many times, I would listen to the same stories echoed from base to base. The men believed that they would never return home alive. It's a strange feeling when grown men believe they are going to die. I could see the sadness in their eyes, eyes of men who thought that they would never see their families again. There were exploded vehicles at every firebase, vehicles which had run over mines and explosives.

It's scary to see these images every day and have the knowledge of all the pain associated with this destruction. But these men continue to fulfill their missions.

There were many things I learned on this deployment that stuck with me. You are the only person who gives a fuck who you are, and, if you want something, you are going to have to get it yourself. This is in the context of being a soldier in the army, of course. All made and missed opportunities were on me. Also, you have to make the best of every day because it might be your last. Indirect fire from 107mm rockets is fast and explodes with a lot of shrapnel. You never forget your green beret while attending a funeral. Lastly, the war was much more complex than I ever knew, and it was tough to understand politics, political power, and the strategic implications of actions and missions.

During this deployment, I attended the army's selection board so that I could be promoted to Staff Sergeant, the enlisted rank of E-6. For Special Forces, this board was much more of a rite of passage than knowledge of information. The board of five senior leaders would ask questions about army policy and regulations, rates of fire on weapon systems, and what the colors on a military map mean. The board made me sing the army song, "Ballad of the Green Beret," and recite the Non-commissioned Officer Creed. I passed the board, and I was recommended to be promoted to Staff Sergeant E-6. I was promoted before leaving Afghanistan in a simple ceremony. I got a handshake and was told by the commander, "Now is the time you start doing work." I headed back to the United States to join my very first ODA.

Marriage saved me from being too self-destructive while overseas, and marriage gave me something to return home for. I had an incredibly beautiful reason to come home.

My wife had endured the worst of me. Shawn heard the stories of horrific events in Afghanistan, the killing of strangers, and the impacts to my mind from the constant fear of death. She lived alone while I was gone. She worked with children with autism and advanced her education by earning a Master's degree in Applied Behavioral Analysis, but she did it alone. She saved money and took care of the house, but most of all, she worried about me. I was not good about calling or writing home. I focused my mind on Afghanistan, the *boys*, and the mission.

My wife was the only one I could talk to about the war and the moral injuries. If I didn't have her to talk to, life would've been so much harder to handle. She had to know who I truthfully was, so I told her everything that happened while I was deployed. Shawn carried the burden of my trauma and her own stuff. Shawn did not have a lot of opportunities to share her problems, so she took on the role of being a caregiver for me. Shawn has always encouraged honesty so that she could support me in the best way she knew how. Her behavior analyst training helped her understand and be patient with me. I lived a compartmentalized life. I was part warfighter and part husband.

———

The *boys* is a term I understood more as I progressed in the military. Some say they are the people to your left and right, or it's a feeling you have when you are bound by a high-stress experience. Others say it's their ride-or-die crew. For me, the *boys* on the block were the players, hustlers, and real OG's, my brothers in combat.

Getting the chance to lead foreign fighters on the battle-field is the height of being a Green Beret. I was able to train and lead Afghan soldiers and Afghan Local Police on an Operational Detachment Alpha (ODA.) I was assigned to 3431, which was the third group, fourth battalion, Charlie Company.

My third deployment was to Western Afghanistan, to a small town north of Farah City named Khaki Safed (KES/KEZ), the nickname for the firebase we lived at. I completed nine months of service at this firebase. KEZ was a remote location far away from conventional army support. This deployment included many of the best and worst experiences I encountered while serving as a Green Beret. I watched people exploding from stepping on mines and IEDs destroying anti-mine vehicles. I saw before gunfights, and I received indirect fire. Direct fire means that the gun can see the target. Indirect fire means the weapons can't see the target.

Our ODA had a main firebase which we used to store fuel and ammunition. We had to keep the firebase secure, and we were in the middle of nowhere. We had built a checkpoint (CP) about ten kilometers away from our main firebase. The ODA leadership would generally send out one Green Beret accompanied by a squad of 19D-Cavalry Scouts, and about three mine-resistant trucks to spend thirty days at the CP.

There were just seven other people in the world that I considered the *boys* at that time—my *boys* in war, the *boys* of KEZ. The *boys* knew the truth about me, and I knew all the truths about them as we operated in the space of ultimate freedom and trust. The *boys* ran the block, watched each other's backs, and could depend on each other. All that we had was each other and guns—lots of guns, explosives, and intelligent minds.

The CP was a village called Nangabad and was considered a "red" area, or non-permissive. This meant that it was under enemy control, and the locals did not have us in their favor. Always under threat, it was a rough place to live and an even worse place to live as an American soldier. Many looked at us as if we were "invaders" and "outsiders". To me, this was the place where a Green Beret should strive to endure.

Many skills needed in this environment were never really taught during the qualification course. I used my trait of compassion. Compassion can help many Green Berets to be a lot more successful with their missions. There was a feeling of attempting to immerse myself in the local population. Learning how to love the communities that we were a part of and the people that we were defending was a huge key for me. This type of emotional attachment to the local communities was never taught but grew from within me. The types of interactions I had with the locals were what it meant to be a Green Beret for me. I went door to door, dropping books, shoes, and radios. I engaged with kids, adults, and the elders of the village.

I lived by buying food and supplies from the local bazaar. The army did provide us with rations, but the rations were not fresh food. The food the army provided came in plastic bags and had a shelf-life of multiple years. By purchasing food from the local economy, I was able to achieve rapport with the local shop owners. These connections gave us a presence in the town. I learned that the Taliban were able to spend twenty-four hours a day amongst the people spreading their dogma, and I had to do whatever I could to combat that time and influence. I would often purchase local meats, fruits, and vegetables from the bazaar for two purposes. The first was for the health and diet of my guys and the Afghans who were living with us. Purchasing locally-procured food allowed us to have dinner together. The second was for the infusion of money into the economy for these local Afghans. This influx of money allowed the locals to build up their businesses and the local mosque.

Months of face-to-face conversations led to a changed view of Americans in this "red" village. We trained and equipped locals so that they could defend themselves against persecution from the Taliban, which also helped change the view of us by the local population. My ODA and its members were able to accomplish a shift from a non-permissive to a semi-permissive environment. We had created some influence over the town where we lived—I was now a true Green Beret.

I knew I was making a difference in the village when I said "hello" to a local man, and he blew me off. I greeted him in the customary way by placing my hand on my heart. I looked him in his old eyes, and he just looked away. This happened in the bazaar where everyone from the village would gather. The people of the village noticed how I was treated. The next day, I went down to the bazaar to make our daily purchase of dinner supplies. As I walked up to the same man, I noticed that he had blood in his beard, and he had a black eye. I asked Rock, our interpreter, what the heck had happened to this guy. Had the Taliban come into his home and injured him? Rock told me, "Yesterday, the old man disrespected you, Trevor." Wait... what? He disrespected me? How?

I realized that the impact of talking to people every day was a cultural norm, and you should always show respect for one another with a return greeting. A huge point of progress in the village happened when locals would pull me aside and tell me the information we needed about the Taliban.

Our CP was a small three-room mud hut. We had a mortar pit with a 60mm, three mine-resistant armored vehicles with .50 cal machine guns, two Claymores, and M240 machine gun nests on top of the building. These weapons and two soldiers would be guards for the CP day and night. Having to pull guard duty became tiresome; standing on the roof with my eyes peeled interrupted my sleep almost daily. But all we really had was each other to make sure that we didn't get ambushed during the day or at night. I would plan and lead all the missions while at the CP, still as a Staff Sergeant. We were in our own little war zone. It was a very compartmentalized life where nothing else existed or seemed to matter.

I was living with one Air Force Combat Controller, or JTAC. This airman had a specialty in communicating with jets and ten up-lift soldier Cavalry Scouts from the 1st Infantry Division at Fort Riley. The up-lift soldier is just an augmentee, or extra body, so the ODA had help in our day-to-day duties around the base and CP.

I would plan many of the missions at the CP during the night shifts. My work would get done on a small computer in a dusty room with a headlamp for a light. I truly received little guidance on what I should be doing. I just made it up and went on missions based on what happened during each day. The next mission I was planning was set to take place in the middle of the night. We were going to walk to the next village south of Nangabad, a town that was supporting the Taliban. Many residents were housing terrorists who were attacking locals, placing IEDs, and ambushing Afghan Army units and US soldiers.

I figured if we could get into the village before the sun came up, we would surprise the enemy prior to the first call to prayer. The local Afghan police were able to get more information for me about what was happening in the village and surrounding areas. We would have the local police move into the town at daybreak to help talk with the locals.

Night-time operations fell into a different category of missions that were not as easy to get approval on. Level zero missions were the easiest to get approval for and had the quickest turnaround. So, I messed with the call-in times when we would start our missions. I was breaking the orders from the higher command when I did this. I just didn't care because I believed that there was no way that the headquarters could find out that we had left. That is, until something bad happened.

The mission consisted of about forty people, twelve Americans, twenty-eight Afghans, a basic army medic, and all-terrain vehicles with machine guns and sniper rifles. We would leave in the middle of the night and walk through the rough terrain. Only the Americans had night vision goggles, which made movement slower, but it wasn't too difficult. I ate Valium like candy as soon as we left the wire. Valium helped keep my anxiety down. I bought the Valium at a local pharmacy from an Afghan shop keeper. I was not authorized to consume these drugs while on active duty. I had a lot of anxiety right from the beginning since I knew we would be off on the mission well before any call-in about the mission would happen. We were outside of the security of our CP, and no one knew we were walking into enemy territory except us.

As we approached the village, I located a building that

had been abandoned and had two stories so that my guys would have an elevated position for machine guns and sniper rifles. This building became our hold-up site, which I would transform into a casualty collection point (CCP). A CCP is a makeshift aid station and location where we could defend ourselves for a prolonged period if things were to get bad. We would occupy the building and set in to rest until sunrise.

As the sun started to rise, I gathered up some of the Afghans, some of the Cav Scouts, and the Combat Controller, and got ready to head into the village. The plan was to walk through the village slowly—we were ready for anything. As we approached the southwestern side of the village, near the mosque, the shit hit the fan.

I walked through an open door and looked inside. There was a huge diesel generator running, smoke pouring out of the exhaust, and a loud humming as the belts of the machine spiraled in circles. I could not hear anything else around me. As I looked back to where I had just come in, I saw dust clouds coming up from in front of the Controller. He stood tall behind a mud wall. Bullets hit the front of the mud wall, and the dust billowed up over the wall. The sun was fully up by this time, so bright it was hard to focus. I walked out the door and looked over my left shoulder into the field where the gunfire was coming from.

I heard troops in contact with the guys around me and on the radio. *Shit!* They yelled, "We need aircraft now!" The CCP had been ambushed as well. Machine guns were sounding on all sides. *Fuck me, it's going to be a long day!*

When I got near the Combat Controller, I told him to contact the higher headquarters and give a situation report about the ambush and our location. I looked out into the field and saw a cemetery to the south. Also, to the west, there were more mud huts and walls that I could bound to. I looked back at the Combat Controller and was mesmerized for a moment.

There are moments in which it's scary to watch a Combat Controller work. They get in *the zone* when talking to aircraft and dismiss their own surroundings. We were being shot at by a PKM machine gun and the Combat Controller was just standing up behind a mud wall as if the onslaught didn't faze him. When you get to see this behavior in action, it is like a conductor directing an orchestra. It was a beautiful thing to witness.

All of us were being shot at, and my CCP was under heavy fire from many separate locations. I had to make a choice to either retreat to the CCP or to close the gap between the Taliban fighter. I looked at the cemetery again and then ran as fast as I could over there to find to cover. As I was running, bullets were impacting all around me. I looked back towards the wall where the Combat Controller was calling in the A-10 to support us—he was still orchestrating. The feeling that there was an A-10, a fighter plane with a huge gun in the center of its body, on its way was a relief. When the A-10 arrives, no one wants to be on the receiving end of this "tank with wings".

I noticed that I was the only person who had run from the wall to the cemetery. As I established cover, I saw an uplift soldier. His eyes were wide open and white, and I noticed he had black hair. *Why can I see his hair?* "Where the fuck is your helmet!? We're getting shot at!" The mud huts and buildings were the next locations, but to get there, I would have to cross the open area again. I went zigging and zagging to the next area of cover. As I ran to the huts, I looked back to see the Afghan police running with me while we were all taking fire. I had gained the trust of these men. I felt like I had earned the Green Beret.

As we moved towards the huts, we moved together over walls and through mud homes. When we reached the last wall, I noticed a Taliban, a machine gunner, about one hundred meters out and off to the side of the road. I could see small grenades exploding around him. These were from handheld grenade launchers. The explosions around him did not seem to faze the enemy attacker.

I yelled out to the interpreter, "Who the fuck is that dude?" To me, it looked as if the gunner was wearing a police uniform, a light-blue jumpsuit-style, so I wanted to make sure that there was no confusion. I pulled up my rifle to get a closer look through my scope. Then, I could hear the shouting, "He's my brother," an Afghan said, and then the interpreter yelled at me. I watched the bullets as they hit the ground around the gunner. I watched the gunner get shot multiple times. His clothes were ripped apart, and he lay still on the ground.

I was quite sure he was dead, but I would clear his body just to make sure. I found detonators and homemade blasting caps near him. This man was making bombs that would destroy our vehicles and cause lots of damage. I took a small amount of C-4 and destroyed the IED-making materials. The chemistry with which these items are made makes them dangerous—they can explode very easily. The Casualty Collection Point had engaged some shooters, but none of our guys were hurt.

As the gunfight died down, I noticed a patrol of Afghans

coming up from the south on the main road. Ghani, the leader of the local police in Khaki Safed District, was coming through the village. I saw the cloud of dust rising from the vehicles and police walking down the dusty road. He told me that his men found an IED in the middle of the main road about a half-mile back. The Combat Controller and I walked about ten meters off the road, and I set up another block of C-4. I used some smoke and line to pull the C-4 over the IED to make it explode. Then, Ghani was able to recover the body of the machine gunner.

Together, we moved back almost shoulder to shoulder, like a football team ready to rush the field prior to the start of a game, to the CCP to recover. I was offered a salty, milky drink. It tasted sour and terrible, but it was an honor given by the Afghans for going into battle, so I drank it all.

This moment reminded me of the time at Robin Sage when we ate the worm. Eating and drinking what is given to you is a sign of respect. I learned this tradition from being around the Afghan people for so many months.

The police and our ODA returned to the CP in Nangabad that evening as the sun was setting. After that day, I was looked at differently. The rough times together grew the brotherhood inside us. Trust another man to watch your back, and he knew you would do the same for him. I just thought I was doing the right thing by trying to keep people safe. That day was exciting and scary. The ambush happened over ten years ago, but I can still remember each detail clearly, as if it happened only yesterday; the screaming, the faces, and the dead persistently returned to my mind and my soul.

Another day that summer, most of my ODA was at the CP when Ghani, the police chief, and the police officers were engaged in a gunfight to the north of Nangabad. My ODA responded to the troops in contact. We moved our three trucks to the site where the fighting was happening. Small trees and brown mud buildings offered cover. As we got closer to the fight, the guys, including our Commander, dismounted from the trucks to support the Afghans in the fight. I stayed in the truck as the .50 cal gunner with a soldier as my driver.

We moved the truck to the south side of the field to act as a cover support element and to cut off a southern escape route. As we advanced, moving along the south flank, we started to receive fire. Keep in mind that we were in an armored vehicle and small arms fire wasn't going to hurt the two of us inside.

My driver started screaming at the top of his lungs and driving wildly. "They're shooting at us!"

"I know!" I said, "And you have to keep the truck steady!" I was sitting in the back of the MTAV, using an automated gunner system to operate the .50 cal. I could see what was happening on the battlefield through a screen, but I couldn't get a clean shot off with the erratic, up-and-down movement of the huge truck on uneven ground.

The driver regained his self-control, steadied his hands, and drove calmly. Muzzle flashes came from the side of a building. FLASH! FLASH! Then, BANG! BANG! BANG! I shot three rounds with the .50 cal into the side of the mud wall where the enemy was firing from. The .50 caliber machine gun was loaded with sabot sub-caliber rounds; this steel-core round had a plastic casing rather than a full metal jacket, which did a better job going through the mud. The firing stopped, the radios went silent, and the screaming ended.

The gunfight was over. We got to the assembly area without any of our people getting hurt.

I sat in the truck, waiting to move back out to the CP and continue to pull security, but I was told I needed to get out of the truck to see the humans I had just killed. There was no need for me to do this. Witnessing the dead bodies offered nothing. I knew what consequences would come from seeing dead bodies. I had a gut feeling that I really shouldn't see the aftermath of the firefight, but I gave in to peer pressure and went against my intuition. I finally gave in and got out of my gunner's seat to view the bodies.

They looked like they had mange. It seemed to me that they hadn't bathed or showered in a year. Their bodies had been searched before I got out of the truck. The items that they carried were next to their bodies on the ground. Amongst the items were IED bomb-making materials, pressure plates, and remote wiring devices, more than I had ever seen before. These two guys were trying to place bombs to destroy our heavy mine-resistant trucks and the Afghan Army trucks we drove around in.

The moral toll that killing people during these deployments would have on me would take about five years to catch up to me. Going to battle with the *boys* was amazing. I understand the compulsion to return to battle, and how it drives us to continue fighting and returning to face the evildoers of the world. There is no other feeling in the world than fighting for your life.

I have relationships with the *boys* that only being side-by-side in war can create. The connection made through war is unmatchable. Many vets think that war and combat are the only thing that gives a human being that unmatchable feeling. Many will spend the rest of their lives trying to feel like that again.

No one was going to help us. No one was going to save us, but us. We had the money. We had the power. And we had the best minds. We had all the resources needed to win in combat. On these deployments, the boys and I earned the respect of many of the Afghan people. Traveling outside of the firebase (village stability site) every day, we would have interactions, many good, but sometimes bad, which was key to earning their trust. We would have good experiences, like handing out food to hungry villagers, and the occasional bad one—once we had to shoot a kid's dog when it attacked us. As the months passed, images from Francis Ford Coppola's film *Apocalypse Now* started to feel as if they represented my life. I had watched the movie while I was back at Purdue when I lived in Theta Xi with a different type of brother.

Being a Green Beret in the middle of nowhere meant having no rules, no morals, no ethics, no care, and no future. I just wanted to treat people fairly and with kindness and compassion. It was a very freeing environment, and it is clear to me how people can miss being in it. We made the rules. Living a life without any set boundaries started to make me feel conflicted—like I was leaning over the edge of a cliff.

Living life in such a precarious way led to a kind of weightless feeling that I'll try to describe. Angling out over the edge, you start to feel your body weight shift. It makes your body want to pull back, so you don't fall off the cliff. Instead of being cautious with your life and realizing that you've gone too far and you might fall, you push farther into the open air, over the drop below, and you become weightless. You see the ground, but gravity isn't pulling you to your death.

Something suspends you. Living in this space for months starts to become confusing because your interpretation of the world has changed from something you have believed in since birth. You know what gravity feels like on your body, but now that feeling is gone.

I took a lot of chances while I was deployed. I am very lucky that I was never physically injured by the enemy. It wore my mind out, though. The constant thinking that the next day might be my last took its toll. The desire to dissociate from the world set in. Emotional pain and sadness also arrived in my mind. I was in a faraway place, all alone for a lot of time.

Thoughts of my wife, Shawn, and being told I wasn't going home again scared me. I could envision her becoming a widow. Her strength and ability to carry on without me was one of the biggest reasons I married her. I knew Shawn would've been able to lead a happy and productive life on her own, but I wanted to share it with her.

Living in Afghanistan created a "you are already dead," kind of complex. Every day, I could die. As the days passed, I began to feel nothing. After months, I just gave up worrying about my life. I accepted that the wish I had made when I joined the army back in December 2000 was going to come true. I was expecting a hero's death.

During this trip, I met Magnus Johnson on the ODA. Magnus left Fort Bragg early to deploy to our firebase in Afghanistan. When I got to Afghanistan, he had already been there for about three months. Magnus was our explosives man and mine clearer. He loved keeping the team safe, and he was amazing at his craft in war. Magnus had been a rough kid who grew up on the wrong side of the tracks. He also had a challenging time with alcohol and drugs. If you were to look at his hands, you would see tattoos that read HOLD on his fingers on his right hand and FAST on his left fingers. He never wore body amour—just a bandana and a cigarette barely hanging off his dry lips, but he always had a rifle slung across his back.

Magnus has a special place in my heart. He was the first American I watched almost be shot dead. Magnus was looking for mines buried in the ground with a mine detector; he was clearing the route for our trucks. He walked in front of all the trucks, scanning over the desert soil, waiting to hear the high-pitched sound that indicated metal on the ground. Every few steps, Magnus would place the detector over his boot where he knew there were metal pieces. He would hear the chirp of the detector and move on. Magnus always tested his equipment; he knew our lives counted on him and his tools. As he was doing the route scan, I saw blooms of dirt bouncing and splashing up around him. It was very similar to throwing rocks in sifted soil.

That moment scared the shit out of me and will be with me for the rest of my life. I loved having Magnus as a teammate, and I almost saw him die right before my eyes. Magnus was on a year-long extension. The IEDs and all the fighting throughout his many deployments eventually wore him out. He'd had enough of the fighting and left KEZ to get out of the army. Magnus had reached the end of his contract and wanted to do other things in his life, to become an artist and father.

The rest of the team was left to keep each other alive. It sucked, but it really made me appreciate everything Magnus had done so the rest of us could live and return home alive. After Magnus returned home, he started making art in the small town of Nashville, Indiana. He built a beautiful leaf sculpture of cast iron titled *Soaring,* near the town's Visitors' Center.

The sculpture was created to bring awareness about veteran suicide. Elder Heart, Magnus's initial nonprofit, was born through a piece of art that consisted of twenty-two huge leaves that looked similar to the ones I had surrounded myself with while I was at Purdue University fifteen years earlier. The *Soaring* piece has two special meanings to me. One is of a younger man who had no sense of war and destruction, and the other, of a husband and father who needed to find his source of life again.

Magnus showed me new meaning, a new perspective, and a better way to live life, that I had so much more to offer.

Leaving Khaki Safed in December 2011 was one of the most relieving moments of my life. I felt like I had beaten that place. I returned home on the nineteenth of December, our two-year wedding anniversary. Shawn and I bought a Goldendoodle named Olive. This small, white fluffball was not the type of dog that I thought we would ever have. But Shawn had been alone, and she needed to have something alive and cozy in her life since I could not be there.

As the days continued, I began to realize that gravity still existed, but it felt new and strange. Gravity now pressed on my mind and body, and all I wanted was to feel weightless again. During my time home, I would prepare to attend the dive school.

My first attempt at military scuba diving school came in July of 2012. I landed in Key West, Florida, on a Friday afternoon, and I didn't have to be at the school until late on Sunday night. I went to the Fly Navy Hotel, checked in, and decided to do the Duval crawl. The Duval crawl is basically drinking at every bar on the famous Duval Street, the main drag strip in Key West. So, I went on a severe binge-drinking expedition for the next few days. I was more focused on partying than I was on being a combat diver. This error in judgment was the beginning of some life lessons that I needed.

On the first day at dive school, you have to take a physical fitness test which consists of push-ups, sit-ups, a five-mile run, and pull-ups. I successfully completed the push-ups and sit-ups. I moved to the pull-up bars completely exhausted. I jumped and free hung from the bar, then began to pull my chin over the bar. These were strict pull-ups with a cadre standing close to you. If you touched the cadre, the repetition would not count toward the seven needed to continue. As I completed my sixth pull-up, I knew I was in trouble; my shoulders were on fire. As I pulled my body up to complete the seventh pull-up, my arms, shoulders, and body just stopped mid-pull. I stared at the bar, wishing I could find the strength, but I was completely exhausted and had nothing else to give. I failed, and it was my fault.

I was on a plane back home that evening. I was upset but I knew that going back to work would be worse. Failing schools in special forces is not accepted well. I received counseling after failing the dive school physical test. I was honest about what I had done, that I had gone out on the town and drank. Being honest made me feel better about the failure. But now I had to start back in training for my next deployment back to Afghanistan.

About two months later, I returned to KES on my fourth deployment to Afghanistan. Leaving home this time was the hardest. I knew that I was going back to the same horrible place I had just left. I was scared for my life.

I knew the land, but I also knew the danger my ODA was getting back into. I was truly scared to return to KES. I cried on the helicopter ride into the base because I was certain I was going to die there.

The pain I felt inside needed to be numbed. I started abusing narcotics daily. As the spike of the needle pierced my vein, I could instantly feel a rush over my body. As if a warm blanket from the dryer was wrapped around me, a feeling of safety and comfort took over my whole body. I lost all the aches and pains in my muscles and joints, but most importantly, in my mind. My mind stopped worrying about dying; I stopped thinking about Shawn. My brain survived off the glass vial; a clear narcotic, Nubain, was what my mind and body now lived for. I stole the ten-milliliter bottles from our medical tent; I also found expired narcotics and, a few times, opium from the locals. The drugs I took were a catalyst to escape from my reality and uproot all the past trauma that I had buried fifteen years earlier.

During my time overseas, narcotics became the way for me to escape from all the trauma that was piling up. Active-duty members of the military need to have an escape while being deployed. The environment had us relying on whatever was around us to survive day to day. For some guys, it was working out, and for others, it was video games or porn; for me, it was narcotics. I would inject them into my left hand, left arm, and feet two to three times a day. There were no traditional mental health services available, and we didn't generally discuss how what was happening around us made us feel. Bravado was a necessity. As you can imagine, these were not the best ways to manage all the traumas we were feeling.

This time, the leadership was more risk-averse than during previous trips to KEZ. Our ODA stayed closer to base. Since we couldn't go out, I stayed in and used drugs. I just wanted to escape—everything. My ODA would shut down KEZ in the middle of the deployment as we were ordered by our Higher Headquarters. The ODA moved to Camp Leatherneck in southwestern Afghanistan. We stayed there for a few months before getting a mission to train Afghan local police in Lashkar Gah, the capital of Helmand Province. After the move from KEZ to Lashkar Gah, we sat around a lot and were not employed in a useful manner. I returned home early so that I could attend a noncommissioned senior leader's course. This course is needed to be promoted to the rank of Sergeant First Class (E-7). I completed the course, and the ODA returned home safely.

I went back to training how to hold my breath and surface swim so that I could attempt to return to dive school later in the year.

On my second trip to dive school, I was all in. As soon as I got there, I signed right into the barracks to get my mind and body right for what was to come in the following six weeks. That Monday morning, I felt prepared and knew there was nothing that would get me to leave early again.

Before I left home, Shawn said, "I didn't marry a quitter, so don't come home unless you pass."

The hardest pool challenge was an event called "lifesaving techniques" which for me felt like "life-changing techniques". It was the only time I ever considered getting out of the pool and ringing the bell which meant I was done and would be going home.

I had crushed dive school until that point, but that day,

I was truly tested. I had to attempt to rescue an instructor while they were trying to use me as a floatation device. It was excruciating and terrifying, and I felt as if I was going to pass out underwater. Panic set in, and I swam away from the instructor for a moment. I collected myself, looked at the quitting bell, and then swam back to complete the event successfully.

I can understand how exhausting this event is for pretty much anyone who goes through it. I've since become a dive instructor and have had to save plenty of students from becoming unconscious during this event. Some of them end up at the bottom of the pool, with me needing to rescue them instead of them rescuing me.

The "one-man comp" that everyone freaks out about was an easy test for me because I had zero fucks to give. I went into a meditative mind state, did what the instructor asked of me, held my breath, stayed calm and didn't panic, and I passed. Celebrations ensued back at Duval Street—binge-drinking at its college best.

I spent four more weeks training during the week and partying on the weekends. On Saturdays, I watched Purdue football in cold, dark bars, drinking beer and eating bad bar food.

FAMILY

Healing, Growth, and the Future

One of the happiest moments of my entire life was the birth of our daughter. None of the killing I had done in my life really mattered until I held my daughter for the first time. Shawn went into labor on April 12, 2014. When the contractions began, we went to the hospital. The events of that evening would change my perspective about being a husband, a father, and about our marriage and love.

Shawn was in labor in a tub full of lukewarm water, and I sat behind her for support during the contractions. Labor lasted for about six hours, and Eleanor came into the world at about 1 a.m. on April 13.

The moment felt as if it lasted an eternity. The connectedness I felt with Shawn was something I had never experienced before in my life. Knowing that we were together when we made her and being together when she was born made me view our love and our marriage in a whole new way.

The birth of Eleanor and the intimate closeness I felt helped us build the foundation for our future happiness. I felt the true meaning of life. Eleanor was perfect, and the love I felt that day was beyond measure. It really felt as if we were all one. I suppose that unity is what a family can feel like.

The time and love required to raise a human are more than I have ever known. The physical and emotional demands are immeasurable. Yes, tougher than combat. I had no idea what I was thinking. My mind was just too full of pain to give any energy to my daughter. When my daughter was born, I recognized how much of an impact the abuse and the war had had on me. I was scared that my daughter would grow up without a father. I was feeling empty. The drinking and the drugs weren't helping anymore. I felt I would be an awful father, but others continued to believe in me.

Before Eleanor's birth, between 2010 and 2014, I spent twenty-five months in Afghanistan. My body had been focused on the team, drinking, training, and staying alive. My mind was just ... somewhere else. The time in Afghanistan changed me. Some changes were for the better, and some were for the worse.

Seeing humans die was hard, but killing those humans seemed justified because of the role I had taken on. By the end of all my deployments to Afghanistan, I had endured a significant amount of moral injury, physical damage to my brain, and plenty of trauma.

Often throughout my life, I had serious thoughts about suicide and about the pain I carried inside. Once I had a family, I thought I needed to keep myself away from these thoughts because I looked at myself as having the disease of suicide and depression that could be passed down to my kids. I shared these thoughts with Shawn, but she always assured me that I would be an amazing father. I kept my suicidal thoughts to myself and suffered in silence a lot. You see, I had convinced myself that my family would be better off without me.

In my mind, suicide was the only way I would be able to avert the destiny I thought my kids would inherit if I stuck around. I experienced continual flashbacks of the horrors from my past, from my childhood all the way up to adulthood. I was heavily burdened by the moral atrocities I'd witnessed and the pain of my childhood.

I was convinced things would be better, and I would be doing the world a favor by removing myself from it. This is a common feeling that I have heard from other combat veterans. This feeling that they see themselves as a "threat" and then wanting to remove that "threat" can lead to poor thinking and choices.

So, with all these dark thoughts in my head, I committed myself to the psych ward at Womack Hospital in Fort Bragg, NC. I knew that I was going to end my own life if I didn't get help. I had convinced myself to at least try to get fixed. There was a small glimmer of hope, but I could barely feel it, and it was even harder for me to believe in it. My mind was fighting my body in a constant battle, and I was tired. My mind wanted it all to end. There was no future or happiness that I could picture myself living. Somehow, my body still had fight left in it.

When I was admitted to Six South at Fort Bragg, I was shown what a new type of leadership in the army looks like. These supervisors listened as I completed my five-day inpatient recovery. There were countless hours of conversation about the quantity of alcohol I would normally consume and the past traumas of my life. I wrote down all the things I was struggling with. Having these things written down scared me because I thought I might never be able to return to a team if anyone found out about my weakness.

After my five-day stay at the hospital, I returned home, and the next level of care began, including working with counselors, social workers, and psychologists. The release from the hospital left me concerned about what my career would look like when I returned to school and then back to an ODA.

I spent a few days at home with Shawn and Eleanor. I talked to Shawn about how I was feeling inside and why I wanted to die. Shawn took my words and concerns seriously. She started worrying about everything that I did outside of the house because she was afraid I wouldn't return home. My actions created trauma inside her, a fear that the one she loved would take his own life.

I knew I was not going to let the system of behavioral health be the end of my career. I needed to find out what I had to do to continue doing what I loved. I had to find my next purpose. That meant getting better and returning to an ODA, then deploying.

First, I knew I had to continue my personal care and get better. Those things were up to me. Second, I needed to learn what "commander's risk" meant. I sat down with health care and mental health professionals and discussed the concept of risk over a few months. Risk became much easier for me to understand and how much one person can impact the mission of the army.

Before this point, I hadn't really thought of suicide as being a risk of leadership. After thinking about the issue more deeply and understanding hazard more, I knew I had to lower my exposure. I knew I had to keep my appointments and put in the hard work on myself. I explained what had happened to me in the past, as a child and as an adult. The discussions included appointments that took me away from the team at times, but the team supported me. The support I received from my colleagues in the 3rd SFG (A) was the finest I have ever had.

When I was released from the hospital, I knew alcohol was a double-edged blade. I was drinking to stay alive, but at the same time, I knew that alcohol was trying to kill me. The problem with alcohol is that it was a tool to help me keep going until the next day, yet, as I drank more and more, the alcohol made it easier for me to give up on life.

Just as I had hoped and worked hard for, after I started my recovery path, I was able to deploy overseas again. Looking back, I now realize that I was getting better for the other Green Berets, the Special Forces regiment, the Army at large, and everyone else except for myself.

Soon after my stay at the hospital, Shawn and I found out that she was pregnant again. The excitement and the joy of bringing another life into this world overtook me. But, even with all the happiness, I still felt cull inside and was afraid that I might not see my second child being born.

Benjamin came into this world on an August afternoon. Shawn had labored at home until she felt it was the right time. We raced to the hospital, checked in, and placed our stuff in a labor and delivery room. Shawn and I knew that we wanted to have another water birth, so the nurse began filling the tub. The water comforted Shawn while she lay against my legs. I sat behind her on the small edge of the tub, my feet soaking in the warm water. I helped Shawn by allowing her to pull on my arms as she bore down to push Benjamin into the world. I saw Benjamin emerge underwater about an hour after Shawn began pushing. When Benjamin was lifted out of the water, he began screaming. I cut the umbilical cord and cleaned him up. He got weighed, his feet were inked, and he was placed in a warm blanket.

In the recovery room, while Benjamin cuddled with Shawn, Eleanor shared with us that she was overly excited to be a big sister and how proud she was of Shawn. Eleanor has looked over her brother since the day he was born. Eleanor became a defender, as well as the gentlest, most caring big sister by making sure he was always bundled up and had a bottle. She even washed his feet.

I completed my Master's degree in Strategic Studies from the National Defense University in July 2016 and returned to 3rd SFG (A). Having a master's degree made me a prime candidate to work in an embassy, or in some kind of State Department role. I was assigned to 1st Battalion Alpha Company where I was hand-picked to work with the French Special Operations Forces in Burkina Faso, West Africa.

I worked at two locations at the Embassy and outside of Ouagadougou for about three months. My responsibilities included helping the French SOF acquire hostile terrorists who had fled Libya. Islamic State terrorists were known to be living and operating around Northern Mali at this time. I would advise and assist the French with their missions within Northwest Africa. I was using my French language skills for the first time since 2008 when I learned it in the qualification course.

Working around Francophones all day provided many opportunities to speak in French. The only problem was that the French speakers wanted to work on their English. There was a good balance between the two languages.

Some missions were cross-border weapons transfers. Other missions involved moving humans across vast areas of land. I would assist in searching for high-value targets with the help of the people at the Embassy.

Throughout this operation, I had conversations with Seal Team Six personnel and the CIA to share actionable data. With my recent education in strategic studies, I had stepped into a whole new arena. I had no formal training in being a collector, nor much of an intel background, but I certainly learned a lot about how the world works during this deployment.

One day, there was a celebration of life event on the compound. A French helicopter pilot had been shot and killed by a terrorist with an AK-47 during a combat engagement. The very next morning, we received intelligence that the number two high-value target had come up on our network. The French and the US worked together to identify his location.

We spent the next twelve hours confirming we had the right guy and the correct location. In time, all our intelligence would be confirmed. The mission was a go, and the French moved their elements towards the target in northern Mali. As the fighting began, images were played in real-time within the Headquarters. We all got to watch the firefight. I listened to the commandos on the radios as they reported the situations that were happening.

The terrorist we were after was causing the biggest threat by shooting at a Cobra helicopter, just like the scenario with the soldier we had memorialized the previous night. No one had the desire for another soldier to be injured or killed. The French pilot engaged the terrorist with a 30mm gun from the Cobra helicopter and killed the terrorist.

As I watched this event unravel, I thought the terrorist had blown himself up, as if he were a suicide bomber like in the videos I had seen in Afghanistan. But what happened was that the thirty-millimeter round hit his head and blew his face off. This was the exact moment I knew I was finished with the killing business.

My deployment was scheduled to last for six months, but I would return home early due to a bulging disc in my lower back. I returned home in mid-January with the idea of moving myself and my family to Key West, FL. I wanted to stop the combat deployments and the killing.

It was my fortieth month of combat in hostile-area deployments. I was exhausted from all the death on all sides. My soul was rubbing thin, and my morality was becoming translucent. There were no boundaries and no right and wrong. I was losing myself and the little bit of humanity I had left inside me.

During this deployment, I couldn't ignore the fact that my daughter, Eleanor, and my son, Benjamin, were now both in my life. I believed that my children would never understand the things I did while I was in the army. I felt I wouldn't be able to talk with them about the things I had done throughout my career. I was scared that I wouldn't be able to show my family love and compassion.

I knew I needed a change, so I decided to request a transfer to Key West to become an instructor at the Special Forces Underwater Operations School (SFUWO.) Six months later, the whole family moved to Key West. Our family move brought even bigger surprises. Key West was about to be hit by Hurricane Irma on September 10, 2017.

Hurricane Irma helped us realize the things we really needed. If it didn't fit into our two cars, then we could likely live without it. We have been a minimalist family ever since, and we value our time with each other much more than any household items.

———

During the years I was deployed, I was never truly present at home. That's a long time not being part of my family. It was a choice that I made. My career mattered more than everything else during those times. I wasn't a good teammate to Shawn. Shawn took the majority of the burden of the household and caring for our two children. Shawn and I were just trying to manage day-to-day life as a family during many of these years.

Being at home was hard for me and having me at home was even harder for my wife, Shawn. Deployments were more exciting than housework and raising kids. I had more of a desire to be "gone" than I had to deal with life and father-hood. Life seemed simpler when I was deployed. I had a lot of power in my hands while overseas that was taken away when I returned home. I just didn't have enough time to fully relax and go through the grieving of war. I think that deeper thoughts about humanity and life as a father and husband would have been helpful to me.

I never took time to reflect on how hard it must've been for Shawn to be alone at home with our two small children. I am sorry that for so many years I never put myself in her shoes. I dragged my wife through four deployments and countless trainings away from home. My wife never quit or gave up on me. I am sorry that she had to be the strong one for so many years.

Sometimes, I was able to put on the brakes and deal with my own issues. Shawn didn't have that luxury. She took on the most thankless job anyone could ever take on, caring for three children—me being one of them. Her hopes and dreams were put on hold. She stopped working in a career that need-ed her to gain experience and face-to-face hours in order to develop her knowledge. I am forever grateful for her choice because there is no way I could've done what she did. I just didn't have what it takes to be a stay-at-home parent.

In Florida, eventually, I started to slow down on the amount of time that I spent at work. Shawn and I were able to catch up on many of the years that I felt had been lost. There was real work that needed to happen if we were going to have a strong family.

After getting married, being deployed, having children, and all the other adventures I experienced to this point in my life, I had a very different understanding of what helped and what didn't help me handle everything I'd endured so far.

First off, I realized that it was okay to not give up on my dreams after the first "no" if the cause was worthy enough. Purdue initially denied my application to attend. Once someone else believed in me more than I did, I was willing and able to give my goal of attending Purdue another shot. You must do your best with the opportunities that are given to you.

Humanity does want to help you. Like the lady in the bursar's office at Purdue, there are many other people who have the capacity to think beyond just themselves and are willing to help you. I encourage you to take a look at many of the resources at the end of this book. Reach out if you need help with many different aspects of your life.

Shawn helped me so much in the early parts of our relationship. I exposed her to the "true Trevor" so that she could know how I really felt inside. Being completely honest with your significant other is something I encourage everyone to do so that you can grow together. Honesty has been the best way for Shawn and me to build the strong relationship we have today. We have to be honest with ourselves and each other. I also encourage you to stop assuming you know what others think and feel about you. Many times, people will be genuinely curious about the honest stories you have to tell.

———

The Q-course was a "long hustle." I developed a plan to achieve my multiple goals of becoming a Green Beret, a combat diver, an expert communicator, and a skillful fighter. Although many of the roads were hard, the goals were achieved, and I was able to largely manifest my destiny. Many of the people who went on to become Green Berets with me suffered from physical injuries, mental injuries, training mishaps, or even suicide. Death seemed to be all around me then, but the many treatments that are available today could've prevented some of these losses.

Watching people around me pass on was something that affected me differently over time. When Sean, my fraternity brother, passed, I had a lot of people around me who were able to grieve openly. We talked about our feelings if and when we wanted to. As time went on and I continued to lose many people around me within the military, I kept my feelings inside, and I didn't share my emotions with others. I definitely used alcohol a lot to try and cope with all of these tragedies.

Losing so many people over my lifetime made me reluctant to make close friends, or to let too many people become close to me. I was scared that if I let anyone in, then they would end up killing themselves, getting blown up, getting hurt some other way, or just moving on with life. I'm now realizing that people are just people, and if we can be aware and respectful of one another in general, then that's a great start. The people at the bazaar taught me this lesson—that everyone has a story to tell and that their experiences have value.

It was extremely difficult for me to stand up to my peers when I knew I was finished with the killing business. Sometimes, being selfish is what's required to make a huge change such as this. Sometimes, being selfish means saving your life along with others. Being brutally honest with yourself and others is necessary for big changes to occur. Big changes were certainly about to happen as I transitioned into a new role as a dive instructor in Key West.

I learned very quickly that boats are hard to drive. They are bulky and move differently, similar to the armored vehicles that I drove while I was in Afghanistan. I just needed time to practice this new skill. I fucked up a lot of hulls, antennas, engines, and props in my first year at Special Forces Underwater Operations (SFUWO). I ran boats into the ground in the flats and filled the engines with sand. Overheated engine blocks and poor tilting methods were all part of the learning experience. In time, I would earn my boat captain's license.

——

The only way I was ever going to be happy was by learning and doing the things that put my mind at rest. I was always thinking about the past, present, and the future all at once. This took a vast amount of energy and time.

I had always known I loved being surrounded by water. Water offered a second world to me; it was a comfort, like a warm blanket around my body. The sea was a new drug that I got addicted to. I didn't know that the ocean would bring peace to my mind, body, and soul. I never thought that going to Key West as a dive instructor for the SFUWO school was going to change my life so much.

When I started to work at SFUWO, I met a group of instructors and coworkers who went fishing and spearfishing often. It seemed like something I could get into as well. I jumped right in and bought a speargun, even though I was unsure if being a "spearo" was something I was going to enjoy. I chose a Riffe Mahogany Competitor, a two-banded gun with a flopper. Its total length is forty inches. It is the beginner shallow reef gun. It's perfect for someone who is new to the sport of spearfishing.

I started spending a lot of time in the water around Key West. I would just park my car and walk into the ocean, which stays on the warm side throughout the year. During the summer, the water stays close to eighty-eight degrees, and at times, it feels like bath water. In the winter, the water gets cold in Key West, and I would then slide on a wet suit which helped keep me warm and protected.

I noticed the saltwater in my mouth the first time I put my face in the water. It's a bit of a shock for some reason. I like to place my face in the water before putting my mask on my face. There was a lot to learn about spearing—breath holding, finning, gear, structures, bait, species of fish, and maps. All these skills took a long time to get right. I needed to be in the water to get better. I noticed that when I was in the water, my memories of the past faded away. I focused on the fish, hunting, and avoiding being hit by boats and jet skiers. Being submerged in the ocean became a form of therapy. It felt peaceful to me, and it settled my internal thoughts.

Mangrove Snapper is the fish that helped me fall in love with spearfishing. My kids absolutely loved the texture and the taste of this simple fish that is abundant in the Florida Keys. They are fun to spear, and the ten-catch limit allows a big haul each day. The scales are dark brown or gray, with reddish or orange stripes on the side and a long black stripe that runs from their nose past their eyes. Like all the snapper family of fish, the Mangroves are very curious and active. They are amazing to watch when they are in large schools in clear water.

I started spearing every day. It was easy on my lower back, and it demanded lots of cardio and breath holding, especially during extreme shifts in current when the ocean would change from high to low tide. The fish and the environment were a great physical and mental challenge for me.

In the ocean, nearly everything can swim faster than you, and creatures might have teeth sharper than any knife you are carrying. These fish clearly have the advantage. What I wanted to learn was how to level the playing field a bit. I strived to be better. I wanted to bring more fish home to my family, and spearing provided me with an adventure—an adventure I had missed since I left Afghanistan four years earlier. The sport was risky, and it provided a thrill, that chemical rush I had chased for so long. I shore dove for about a year before I felt comfortable identifying the species and as I became a more experienced boat driver. I started by going out to the reef now and then, along with a few blue water trips with guys from the school. Most of the time, I was swimming against the current, waiting for a fish to swim by. This was the start of falling in love with spearing.

Shawn and her best friend Devon believed that the men in their lives needed to become best friends. Shawn had signed up for the Key West CrossFit competition, the first one she had ever done. Shawn said she was going to work out as a team with a man named Curtis, Devon's boyfriend. Curtis Dean Kellam should be known as the "asshole friend". Curtis showed up late or never. He had an awful attitude and hated other people. Some would call him "Doc Holliday", just like the character from the movie *Tombstone*.

I wanted to support Shawn and her teammate whom I had never met. I was super pumped for Shawn because I knew this competition was important to her. Shawn had been doing CrossFit since 2011, but she had never committed to doing a competition. I wanted her to have an enjoyable experience so that she would continue competing.

Key West is extremely hot in the summer. Luckily, the competition was held at the local outdoor roller-skating rink which was covered. The sun didn't beat down on you as it usually did. Shawn left the house early to go warm up. The kids, now four and two, got ready to go watch her compete. We arrived a little later than expected because I was trying to figure out how to get two kids out of the house on my own. I was afraid that I would do something wrong; I had to check over everything twice before leaving the house.

As we walked up to the roller-skating rink, I noticed a guy with a completely black tattooed right arm, sweating more than anyone else, on his back slamming a beer. *Who the fuck is this dumbass?* We kept walking to the stands, only to witness a bald guy in a kilt screaming into the microphone. This was not the CrossFit I was used to back in North Carolina.

All the weirdness we were seeing ended up being quite normal for the Conch Republic. The Conch Republic is a nickname for Key West. A group of residents had declared a sarcastic withdrawal from the United States on April 23, 1982.

Shawn made her way over and let me know that her partner was kind of drunk and kind of hungover, too. *Who gets drunk the night before a competition and then continues to drink before the competition?* Shawn pointed the guy out to me. Yup—the one who looked like he was having a heat stroke but was still drinking a beer, was Curtis, her teammate.

What a fucking dumbass! It goes without saying that we witnessed a godawful attempt to perform by Curtis. Shawn was simply happy that she didn't have to push too hard. Curtis tried to live up to his word. He had told Shawn that he would be her partner, but he never said that he would be sober, rested, or hydrated.

Over the following months, Curtis became my friend. He was an army veteran with deployments to Iraq and Afghanistan. He grew up around Virginia Beach, but never really spoke about his childhood except to say that he enjoyed skating. Curtis and I would spend time drinking and conversing about the future and how many kids he wanted to have with the love of his life, Devon.

Curtis had left the military, expressing great disappointment in its leadership. He had been deployed with the 82nd Airborne to Helmand, Afghanistan and fought bravely alongside his teammates. Curtis held many memories inside. I learned he had difficulties with his previous wife and had battles with physical pain. He had broken his hand in a training accident.

The most hidden part of Curtis was his anxiety. He would put himself in a bad place by drinking and not showing up for work. This dude made it seem as if he didn't give a fuck about life. He had a "Cool story, Bro" type of attitude and an off-the-cuff type of lifestyle. Curtis would roam the streets of Key West, riding a matte-black beach cruiser with no shirt on, flip flops, and a Bud Light in a koozie on the handlebars. If you ever saw Curtis riding, then you saw a guy swerving left to right in the middle of the street without a care in the world. He was either drunk as fuck or just flying through life. You never knew with Curtis.

He usually had a mouthful of Copenhagen and was always on the move. He was always trying to find his phone or fix his broken-down Chevy Suburban. It felt as if Curtis never slept. To me, Curtis seemed like a beaten-down, sad bulldog at the pound. Everyone said they wanted him, but to take him home was too risky for most because you just didn't know his past, which made you question if he would ever bite.

Curtis was the type of guy who could live off pickle juice and street meat. Even though he was hurting inside, he found love in his heart for my kids. Curtis would buy the worst gifts, the type of gifts parents hate. It was either the toys that made a lot of noise, or they would break within thirty seconds. Curtis was a friend who would stay at your house *well* past his welcome. Shawn would pull me aside and whisper, "When is he going home?"

But we were his home, and I felt sad when he left because he was someone who understood what I felt. Curtis made me feel normal within my own skin. He was relatable. Curtis worked his ass off at everything but was really shitty with economy of motion. If you ever saw him lift weights or do CrossFit, then you would understand how painful it was to watch. Curtis had zero technique in a sport that required lots of skill, heart, brawn, and zero quit; bloody hands and vomit were common.

When Curtis and I were together, it seemed normal to drink three cases of beer during the day then slam Jameson whiskey shots at night. I wanted to get as drunk as I could after the kids were off to sleep. One of the things it took me a few weeks to realize was that Curtis would drink alcohol all day long before we started drinking in the evening. I would try to get him to drink faster, not noticing that he was already smashed.

During the hottest times of the summer, we spent time by the pool, at the ocean, in bars, and on boat rides. Curtis would have a Bud Light in hand and a dip in the side of his lip. Curtis was always willing to fight and would never quit. Doc Holliday only had one true and genuine friend—me. I know Curtis would have fought for me if I ever asked him to. He would have given his life to protect my wife and children.

———

In late 2018, I walked out of my house in Key West with the intention of never coming back home. The feelings from years earlier when I felt my family would be better off without me were resurfacing. My mind was telling me I would be a failure as a father and a husband. The intensity of the trauma I had held since I was a kid and from the war was at an all-time high.

To cope, I was drinking alcohol constantly and working long hours at the Army dive school. Eleanor and Benjamin were only four and two years old; raising the kids was hard on my wife because I wasn't there to help out.

I wrote Shawn a letter and put it on the microwave door. The letter said, "Goodbye, tell the kids I love them." I left the house to go and drink my life away. My plan was to fade away into the ocean and just be gone—to get lost at sea and never be found. Somehow, my mind made sense of this thinking. I was in a very dark place, and I didn't care about anything.

After Shawn found the note, she reached out to some of my co-workers and friends to help find me. She was frantic, calling everyone in her phone and waiting for the answer that I had been located. Within a few hours, Shawn was notified that I was safe. She was able to calm down, but the fear of me not returning home still plagues her to this day.

Every time I got to the point of wanting to die and escape, I was drunk. When I was overwhelmed with life and stressed out, I responded by guzzling alcohol and then wanting to hurt myself. While intoxicated, I lost my love for my body and thought punishing myself was the only way to feel better.

One of the problems with being committed to marriage was that I couldn't quit. My marriage was another thing that I wanted to prove I could do better. I didn't know how to have conversations without having emotional responses. I didn't possess the ability to think about situations critically; instead, I felt like I was being personally attacked.

I really hadn't been shown what a good marriage looked like as I was growing up. As a kid, I was taught to stonewall problems and that time would make everything get better and go away. This is not a coping strategy that anyone should adopt and use in their life. By doing nothing, nothing will ever change or get fixed. It took a lot of practice expressing how I felt to get past the stonewalling technique of conflict resolution.

In June, as I approached my second year as a dive instructor, I attempted a deep dive certification for a Combat Diver Course. This dive was scheduled to be 130-feet deep off the USS Vandenburg, which is a shipwreck located a few miles to the east of Key West in the Atlantic Ocean.

The sea state was wonderful that day. There were low winds and maybe a one-knot current—the conditions felt perfect. I'd had the chance to dive the wreck once before, in 2013, while I was in dive school, and was excited to dive the site again. I conducted the dive the same way I had done it in 2013. I reached the surface, reported the depth and time, and that I felt fine. I thought everything went great.

I removed my scuba tanks and drove back to Key West, feeling no pain and without any concerns. I got back to base, cleaned my gear, showered, and went home for the evening.

I was sitting on the couch at home watching our son Benji jump up and down and run back and forth on the couch. I watched his little feet move so fast to try to keep up with his slender, chicken body. Benji's white-blonde hair bounced all around as he jumped, and he wore only blue shorts over his bronzed skin.

I felt something weird in my right femur, like a screw was slowly being driven into the bone, but without touching any of the muscle. It was a weird ache that I had spoken and learned about while teaching diving but had never experienced myself. I gently rubbed my skin but couldn't feel the touch of my fingers. *Oh, fuck me!* It had only been two-and-a-half hours since I had surfaced from the dive.

I yelled for Shawn and told her that there was something

wrong. She asked if I had called the doctor yet. *Nope! Shit!*

Doc Ambroson, the medical diving officer, was on speed dial because a medical officer was required to be on call for all the diving that we conducted. "What's up, Trev?" Doc had a wonderful relationship with all of us at the school. Doc was a person I had talked with about suicide and substance abuse. He always supported me and the ways that I wanted to get help.

I gave Doc a quick rundown of my symptoms. No more than fifteen seconds into the conversation, he told me to get my ass to the dive chamber. "Trevor, you are getting pressed, and you might be in there for a while." I was headed for the hyperbaric chamber to try to release the bubble from my leg bone before it caused a stroke. The hyperbaric chamber allows a person to get to depth without having to dive in water.

I knew I would be at least five hours in the chamber. The Navy Dive Manual explains the different types of diving injuries. With each injury, there is a specific amount of time that the diver has to spend at depth in the recompression chamber.

I didn't have a full understanding of how dangerous getting bent could be. Having a stroke underwater is not an ideal situation. The bubble could've stopped anywhere in my body. I was lucky it was inside my leg. I was running low on extra lives. I had cheated death once again!

I made it to the chamber in only eight minutes, but the thoughts of what was going to happen to me were racing at one hundred miles per hour. Would this aching pain go away? Would I ever feel my leg again? After a quick seven-minute neurological check by a dive medical technician, I was subsurface in the chamber. The technician increased the pressure to make my body react as though I had descended to sixty feet. I breathed pure oxygen for an extended dive that took approximately eight and a half hours.

Two people I remember being with me throughout this ordeal were Matt and Mark. Mark assumed the role of medic in the chamber so that he could take my vital signs and help ensure I had medical assistance. Matt drove the chamber. The driver controls the depth—many feet per second—and when carbon dioxide builds up in the chamber, vents the chamber so that the medic and I had good air to breathe.

Matt was the timekeeper and the voice I heard over the intercom. He never left throughout the entire dive simulation. The chamber is a cold, steel tube, with stainless benches to sit on that can hold eight people. There is an additional chamber attached to the side so that people can come and go without having to take the patient to the "surface" each time someone needed to leave or be switched out. The medics who oversaw me changed out every few hours.

One medic stayed inside the chamber with me for the duration of the dive. Mark and I watched *American Psycho* on a cell phone with no audio because it was on the outside of the chamber. Electronic devices can possibly create a spark and cause a fire. The phone was laying on a small porthole. Our conversation was cheerful, and the comments about the movie ended up being more of a back-and-forth banter. Watching Christian Bale murder people helped to pass the time.

The chamber was hot and then cold. It was all steel and plastic. You could either lie or sit on a stainless-steel bench. It was not comfortable. There were no blankets or pillows due to them being combustible; a fire inside the chamber would be extremely dangerous.

I had another big challenge to face. Prior to this dive injury, I had agreed to head to rehabilitation because I wanted to stay on active dive status. I was already being treated by a Veteran's Affairs (VA) doctor for suicidal ideation, PTSD, depression, and alcohol abuse disorder. Alcohol abuse disorder is a fancy way of saying that I was an alcoholic. Dive status in the army is governed by the Navy Dive Manual in terms of regulations. The Navy regulations state that a diver diagnosed with alcoholism must attend treatment for substance abuse disorder or be taken off dive status.

After getting released from the chamber, I was referred to a cardiologist. I received a diagnosis that had a large impact on my future as a diver. A Patent Foramen Ovale (PFO), or a hole in the heart, is a condition that a diver who is going to use compressed gas ought to know about prior to diving. The PFO increases the amount of nitrogen the body absorbs because the gas is passing across the heart, and the nitrogen accumulates in the body at a faster rate than someone without a PFO.

A diver with a PFO has an elevated risk of decompression sickness. As a diver with a PFO ascends towards the surface at the correct rate of speed, their body cannot remove the nitrogen quick enough due to an over-concentration. Hence, when a diver with a PFO surfaces, there is a greater risk of a bubble getting stuck somewhere in their body, most often in the joints.

Well, after finding out that I had a PFO, I didn't want to go. I had only agreed to attend the Naval substance abuse and rehabilitation program so that I could continue to dive. Because diving was now out for me, I had an attitude of "fuck rehab".

In actuality, I needed rehab for me and my family. I made a choice for myself. I knew it was going to be hard, and I would have to admit a lot, but I expected a lot in return. If the Navy wanted to take me away from my family for a month, then it had better be the best program I'd ever been through. It wasn't, and it almost cost me my life.

About two weeks after the Fourth of July, I attended the Navy substance abuse and rehabilitation program. This time felt different. I clearly needed help, and I was honest about how I felt. The first few days at the center, I attended classes on the impact of alcohol on the body and on the outcomes of alcohol misuse. The education and skills being taught to me seemed very basic and not very useful. I was able to leave the barracks to attend Alcoholics Anonymous and to get dinner. As I drove around the city with no purpose or direction, I started feeling like I was looking for the right tree to speed my rental car into to kill myself, rather than finding a way to get home. Dying and death were the only things my mind could understand—no wife, no kids, no family and no army. I hadn't been this highly suicidal since I was twelve years old. I had only felt this hyper-suicidal when I had been binge-drinking for multiple days in a row. At this point, I had been without alcohol for seven days.

This time, I was sober. The world and my mind were dark and emotionless. The only thoughts I had were about killing myself. The feeling that the world would be better without me returned. I couldn't picture a positive future life, or any future at all. I knew my children would be better off without me in their lives. My mind was convinced that killing myself was the only answer to stop the pain and suffering.

Being sober yet still having the overwhelming desire to

die was beyond scary because I had thought that alcohol was the single factor that was trying to kill me. I didn't think it was me. *I* couldn't be the reason I wanted to die.

The same day I considered driving my car into a tree, I spoke up to my counselor. I told him that if I was not admitted to the psych ward that day, he would never see me again.

I was transferred from the Jacksonville Naval Hospital psych ward to the Emerald Coast Behavioral Hospital (ECBH) in Panama City. My own crisis and eventual transfer occurred just before my dear friend Curtis took his own life. This may have been because he knew I was in a safe place in the hospital, but we will never know for sure.

Getting to ECBH involved a three-hour ride in the back of an ambulance, on a stretcher, in the middle of the night. I remember mostly staring out the window as other cars went by. The ride was uncomfortable, but I was happy to be out of a place full of crazy people. At least I was able to call my family and friends from the ambulance.

The ward and ECBH had limited phone access and no internet. These restrictions were supposed to reduce triggers and distractions from the treatment path.

I was pleased to be moving to a new place where I thought I might be able to get some help. The doctor at the Naval Hospital told me ECBH was a multi-track facility that would be able to help me with the various problems I had. I thought that I would have my own room, be able to make my own schedule, and have plenty of time to rest.

I was a bit misinformed about where I was headed. I was told that I would be working on a dual diagnosis track, when, in fact, I had all four tracks: mental health, combat trauma, sexual trauma, and trauma-related illness.

I arrived in the middle of the night, and processing took a few hours before I could go to the military wing of the hospital. Back when I was in college, I had been processed into county jail for public intoxication; being processed into the treatment center felt very similar. Everything was searched. I was given a drug screen, and the results showed zero drugs present. It had been months since I had taken drugs and ten days since I had drunk alcohol. Next, all the laces and strings from my clothing were removed.

I was not prepared. I didn't have the correct clothes. The athletic shorts I brought to Jacksonville were not the ones I would have chosen to bring to Panama City. This wasn't a huge problem, but small things were very aggravating for me in my unstable condition.

I received my toiletry items from the nurse's station: shampoo, a plastic bucket, toothpaste, a toothbrush, and a water bottle. A gentleman walked out of his room from behind me. I turned to look at him and noticed he was pale and that the words he was speaking didn't make any sense. He began to walk closer to me, but his eyes rolled back in his head, and he fell and hit the floor.

I turned to the nurse, "Ma'am, what the fuck is this? I think this dude needs some help!"

The drugs people were prescribed at Emerald Coast could have adverse effects that fucked with their sleep and cognitive responses. The hospital was actually very good at adjusting the drug dosages of the patients while trying to find the perfect match for their symptoms. However, I felt like I had just arrived at the crazy house; people were just falling out in front of me! My recovery journey had begun.

Sixty days after beginning an intense inpatient recovery

program, I was able to see that alcohol was just the fuel for the fire that was inside me. This fire wanted to consume all the oxygen I had in my lungs as I tried to pull myself from the bottom of the ocean.

Some of the methods used to help get me better while at Emerald Coast included Cognitive Behavioral Therapy (CBT), Cognitive Processing Therapy (CPT), Eye Movement Desensitization and Reprocessing (EMDR), SMART recovery, and Alcoholics and Narcotics Anonymous.

———

Do people have to be taught how to love themselves? At one point in my life, I loved living. The abuse from my stepfather took my self-love away. The trauma of sexual abuse acted as a precursor to my abuse of drugs and alcohol. I struggled to understand this for a long time, but rather than feeling pain, I just felt nothing.

The use of drugs and alcohol changed how I felt and how the world around me felt. Did happiness come from something else? Because I sure as hell couldn't have fun and feel good without drugs and alcohol. This last statement was a lie that I believed and turned into truth over time in my mind and body.

I really didn't know who I was inside and what I wanted to do with my life. I looked at myself as kind of soulless—like somebody who didn't have a good future.

Doctor Roy Deal was the man who put me back together. He was white-haired, a bit overweight, with pale skin and a calm but stern voice, the exact type of doctor that fits in at a mental institution. Dr. Deal had been working with trauma in his patients since 1989. This guy had seen it all—he had worked with over 17,000 inmates and countless military service members, veterans, and civilians. Dr. Deal is the real deal when it comes to understanding the impacts of trauma and the way that medicine and therapy can help people live a better life.

I did not work directly with Dr. Deal every day. He oversaw the operation, and his nurses and clinicians were responsible for completing the work.

My intensive therapy started with writing a lot and talking in groups about my past. I focused my efforts on my childhood sexual abuse. Reading and writing about events in my past brought a lot to the surface. The images and feelings from my past were becoming more and more present in my mind. I lived in my trauma all day long. This was very painful and caused awful migraines. My temples felt as if they were being hit by a sledgehammer while also being squeezed in a vice. Loud noises and bright lights were painful to see and be around. I felt cut off from the world.

Limited use of a cell phone and the internet made me spend more time thinking about myself. All week was spent in groups talking about my past. I cried all the time. Finding my purpose to keep on living was harder to see at first.

Cognitive Behavioral Therapy (CBT) and Cognitive Processing Therapy (CPT) were presented in a group setting. Each session would have different topics, and the attendees would generally have similar experiences based on that topic. Some meetings would focus on combat veterans, parents, and people with a history of childhood trauma and addiction.

Everyone sat in a circle and had conversations about topics led by one of the social workers. I enjoyed these meetings because I liked to listen to other people and what they had been through in their lives. At times, these sessions were hard for me to attend. I didn't agree with all the methodologies or treatment styles, but the most encouraging factor for me was the commitment of the other people to open up about their struggles.

I also attended Alcoholics Anonymous. The patients who had problems with alcohol addiction would run these meetings. This was my first exposure to AA and the "Twelve Steps", and it helped me think a lot about my recovery. I didn't feel like I got a lot out of the meetings, but I was able to read parts of "The Big Book" and learn from the stories of other people who struggled with alcoholism. The beginning of the Serenity Prayer was the most important takeaway from these meetings for me. I would replace the word "God" in my head with "myself."

"God, grant me the serenity to accept the things I cannot change, the courage to change the things I can, and the wisdom to know the difference."

Additionally, I would attend Narcotics Anonymous (NA) meetings, which were also self-run. ECBH would sometimes bring in people from the community to run both the AA and NA meetings. I felt a closer connection with the people who had a narcotic addiction than with those who had an alcohol problem. The stories and feelings of the patients in NA were just more relatable to me. The pain of searching for the next fix of opiates and constantly thinking about how to get drugs again was much more relatable than the desire I had to drink alcohol. I drank to forget, and I used drugs to feel no pain.

I also attended something called SMART Recovery. The acronym stands for Self-Management and Recovery Training.

SMART is a newer recovery approach which is very different from the twelve-step method of AA and NA. SMART is based on scientific methods rather than on spirituality, with a heavy emphasis on self-empowerment, cognitive behavioral techniques, and coping with cravings. Rather than focusing on alcohol use as the only issue, SMART methods are meant to help resolve underlying issues surrounding addiction.

The SMART Recovery program is run by a non-profit organization and centers on four points:

1. building motivation
2. coping with urges
3. problem solving and
4. lifestyle balance.

I enjoyed the SMART methods much more than AA or NA. My lack of faith in them was a major reason why AA and NA would not be successful programs for me. SMART taught me how to better navigate the problems I was dealing with and work on the issues that caused me to use drugs and alcohol. This option was just better suited for who I am and what I believe in. The SMART program for recovery allowed me to have more power over myself rather than having a big emphasis on God.

Throughout my stay at ECBH, I attended many therapy sessions covering a vast range of topics. The most impactful talk therapy session I had was with a veteran's group. There were active members and retirees who would speak about their time serving, but also about their lives prior to and post-military service as well. I would speak in detail about my childhood, my background, and my military service.

People gave me the nickname "The Philosopher" while we were all in the ward. I like to talk, and I would talk a lot.

I tried to speak in such a way that people could understand how I felt. Over time, expressing myself easily became a strength.

I believe that you can explain everything you experience in your life. Storytelling takes practice to find the right words to describe what you see and feel. It can be very painful, and being vulnerable can be difficult, but with time and practice, the storytelling process becomes much easier.

The pain didn't seem to feel as bad over time. I will always cry at certain parts of my story, and there is nothing I can do about it. It just impacts me with so much emotion that I can't even hold back the tears. I *want* tears to come out. I view tears as part of the healing process and as an expression of honesty. The Army provides an ethos: *I will always place the mission first, I will never accept defeat, I will never quit, and I will never leave a fallen comrade.* In a way, I felt as if I was falling away from the commitments which had been instilled in me over so many years. Crying was not something I saw in the warriors that surrounded me. I don't see crying as a weakness—crying is a connection to your heart, soul, and mind. Crying is part of the pain of life, and everyone has pain.

———

People have told me that they heard positive messages while listening to me speak. The stories I tell can impact a lot of people. The participants in the veteran's therapy sessions were the first to suggest that I write this book. I had never thought there was any worth to the story of my life, let alone the traumas I had gone through.

One day, two men asked me if they could have a moment to speak with me alone. Each of them told me that watching me have the courage to tell my story helped them finally talk with someone about their childhood sexual trauma.

One vet was in his 60s, and the other was in his 40s. One of them was raped by another man when he first joined the military. Both told me that they had never spoken of their trauma before. They expressed gratitude that a Master Sergeant Green Beret, a decorated soldier, a husband, a father, and an addict, was able to share the hardest things in his life. They said that I was empowering and gave them the strength to say the words abuse and assault for the first time. I never knew what my story could do to help other people.

Eye Movement Desensitization and Reprocessing (EMDR) is a long process in which the patient must relive the events of trauma in their mind and body. As if being put through the worst events of my life wasn't enough the first time, I was about to live them all again.

I was encouraged to write about the most vivid moments of abuse by my stepfather. I would think about every single object in the room. I remembered how the waterbed moved. I heard the vibrator and the way that it felt. I could remember the curtains and the dresser. There was a dim light. I kept my eyes shut and would only dare to peek occasionally to see what was happening to me.

The process of remembering the past so vividly was extremely painful. The intrusive memories hurt and caused me to have harsh migraines. I did EMDR in a small room with a female therapist. When I started the treatment, it was hard to say the words I was seeing in my mind. Describing what I was seeing is very much like seeing a painting that is three-dimensional. The painting shifts from black and white to the most vivid colors of a kaleidoscope. It's very hard to capture all the shapes and colors because the picture is a full-motion movie. It was hard talking to a woman about the things that had happened to me. It was extremely difficult to describe being raped and ejaculated on. It was worse than being shy or embarrassed. I am a man and a Green Beret, and I felt disgusted in my own skin.

I had to remind myself that other people were making sacrifices for me to get better. Being this type of therapist must have impacted her life and view of the world. I needed to stand up for myself and just not give a fuck about how I thought my story would make others think about me. So, I did it. I got fully immersed in the art of being true. The truth, you see, may also set others free, too.

The words I finally spoke lit the way forward for me. I had kept the raw memories inside my mind and body for over thirty years. I had never spoken in depth about the details of my childhood trauma. I had never described in depth the progression of the abuse and the times I actually enjoyed it. It was both pleasure and pain—my mind and body loved them both.

At eight years old, being touched was sometimes a pleasure beyond anything I had ever experienced. Sometimes, it felt wonderful, and my mind would tell me I wanted more. These complex feelings were the hardest to openly talk about in the groups and in private EMDR sessions. Sometimes, I felt that I wanted the abuse to happen. Sometimes, I felt as if I would position myself at night so that I could help make it happen. It's hard to say and to admit, but it's the truth. Sometimes, I just really enjoyed being touched.

The therapist would start the EMDR sessions by asking me to bring a specific childhood traumatic moment into my mind. She would wave a single hand with two fingers in front of my face about two feet away, and I would track her fingers as they moved back and forth. This would last for about 20 to 30 seconds. The "set" or placement that I created for my memory looked like a drive-in movie theater. I would sit in the driver's seat of some kind of 1950s-looking convertible car. I would have the horror story playing on the big screen. I was able to move the car closer and farther from the screen in my mind.

The images would flash on the screen at first, and over the sessions, the movie would become more fluid and more intense. The perspective changed—sometimes, I was in my body reliving it; other times, I was a bystander next to the bed. Still other times, it was as if I was watching the scene in a movie theater. I would feel sensations in my body as I watched the film playing on the screen. It was an eerie feeling. It felt like a warmth and pressure inside my body and on my skin. My therapist would ask me to change the picture to black and white then back into color. She would ask me to focus on the surroundings and then explain what was happening to the child on the screen. I would explain everything the best way I could and use as many details as possible. Everything I explained, I saw and felt as if it were happening in the present.

These sessions would each last about ninety minutes and took a physical and mental toll that left me completely drained. The migraines I would get after these sessions were so intense that I could barely open my eyes. I would lose my appetite, and all I wanted to do was sleep. I would get a shot of Promethazine, which would help me sleep. I think I got this shot three different times during my stay at the hospital—

it allowed me to break the migraine and get about eighteen hours of sleep to recover.

Sleep was the cure for the EMDR sessions. Getting enough sleep allowed my brain and body to process the reliving of the trauma and place it in a section of my mind that felt like a long-term memory zone. The memories and intrusive thoughts started to fade away.

Sleep aids like Trazodone would not allow my mind to reprocess the memories and the events that I had relived during treatment. The Trazodone ruined the work I had done in session. I only took the sleep aid for one night, and I knew when I woke up that I had set my recovery back a day.

There were a few times throughout my stay at ECBH when I felt as if I was being sucked down into the darkest depths of my hell. This deep, dark place housed the same feelings I experienced when I was at the highest peaks of my suicidal mind. Prior to EMDR, I constructed a safe place in my mind to return to if I had gone out too far. I built a boat in my mind. This coping mechanism of pulling myself into the boat has been a priceless tool that I have continued to use. Jumping into the boat pulls my mind out of the destructive thinking it can get caught up in. It's like a snap between reality and the false thinking of my mind. My mind now has the ability to stop the path of self-destruction, but I needed to be taught this skill. I would never have been able to do it on my own.

I was able to build this safe place because of the very vulnerable EMDR work. While I was doing these sessions, I was taken to places that were definitely dark and scary for me. When I would get too far gone, it felt as if death was taking over my body. Everything turned black. There was nothing. There was nothing to live for or care about; it was just dying. So, my therapist helped me to create a safe place in my mind.

Picture being in the middle of the ocean. There are no clouds in the sky, and you can see down at least one hundred feet into the crystal clear water. Birds are flying overhead about 1,000 feet up. But, simply being in the middle of the ocean wasn't going to work. I needed more. *A boat!* Let's build a boat in my mind surrounded by the most peaceful place I know, a calm ocean.

The ocean doesn't care who or what you are. It has wonderful mythology associated with it. Pirates, drifters, and adventurers have all been called to the ocean. The truth I feel about the ocean is that it will eat everything, and it has no feelings. The ocean is dark, but it's alive, and some think it has a memory.

My boat had to be built to stay afloat on the ocean. Day by day, I would mentally piece the boat together. It had an outer, white, fiberglass hull, but the bow and stern were layered with teak, so that it had a swirl to the texture. My boat was freshly stained, detailed, and cleaned. The wood glowed in the sun. The engines were very quiet and never seemed to emit any smelly exhaust. As I stood in the center of the boat, it drove itself—I was just a passenger.

The boat moved while I was aboard. I could feel the wind going through my hair and taste the salt on my lips. There was a calming noise I would hear as the hull sliced through the water. The state of the weather would change depending on how I felt. If the conditions were not favorable, that indicated something about how I was feeling.

I can remember one instance during EMDR where I was

staring at my eyes in the mirror in my parents' bathroom. I watched myself slit my wrists and down the pills. Seeing my face reminded me how much I had wanted to die. Those feelings rushed through my body, and I couldn't stop crying. I could feel the fear overcome me. I think the therapist could sense something was wrong. She told me to go to my safe place. I was surrounded by black emptiness as I tried to direct my mind to the boat. I didn't know which way was up, and I couldn't see any bubbles, but I felt as if I was moving through the depths of the ocean. The therapist repeated to me to get to my safe place, and I worked even harder to force my mind out of the ocean. As I began to surface from the dark depths, I could feel the ocean moving faster past my fingers, face, and ears.

I began to see light shining from the sun, streaking through the ocean and piercing through the depths. The white hull of the boat became clearer and more noticeable. I could finally make out my hand which was positioned above my head to protect me as I surfaced. The water started to come to life with schools of fish swimming around, but they weren't startled or scared of me.

As I got closer and closer to the bottom of the boat, I could feel the fear inside me fade away. Peace and calm came over my body. I stretched to grab hold of the boat, got on, and was soon gliding over the flat, calm ocean. There again was the wind, the sun, my breaths, and peace.

My boat has been a helpful tool when I have felt overwhelmed. It is something I can use anywhere at any time. The technique has taken a little practice, but it has helped me avoid moments when, in the past, I would've used alcohol to drink away my feelings. It's like my own little booze cruise, but without the hangover.

I was wrapping up my stay at Emerald Coast and only had a few days left before I was set to return home. I was approaching sixty days of being away. I had completed many hours of various therapies and skill-building in preparation for post-rehab living. My last EMDR session was surprising. I didn't understand that I would be guided on a journey through internal mind recovery.

Going through EMDR felt like being in a deep sleep and dreaming that I was peeing on myself. The warmth of the urine felt so real. That warmth was similar to the feeling of being touched.

The warmth I felt was hard for me to understand. I could feel the sensations on my face, penis, chest, and anus. So, how could this make for an effective close-out session? I'm hopeful I've been able to explain the feelings that EMDR created in my mind and body. It was very powerful, but also very painful at the same time. I don't recommend someone doing intense EMDR outside of an inpatient medical center. The treatment made me feel very suicidal and depressed. I was not a fun person to be around because I was feeling very aggravated and hateful.

It was hard for me to see the end of EMDR, but I wanted the pain to go away. I feared every session of EMDR, and the work made me want to kill myself. Before the last session, my anxiety was through the roof. I wanted to avoid the memories. However, the months of sessions had started to make the memories less painful. It's as if the knife of those memories had become less sharp, and they couldn't slice through me as easily as they once could. The memories were still present, but they just didn't hurt as badly anymore.

As the last session continued, I tracked the slow movement of the therapist's fingers as before, but the questions were much different than in past sessions. The questions revolved around picturing my family, surrounding myself in a peaceful area, and seeing myself returning home. These images were brighter and more colorful than anything I had put together throughout my previous sessions.

There was a vast green field with a white house sitting at the top of a gradual incline. My wife and two kids sat on the porch in rocking chairs, swaying back and forth. It was as if I was viewing them from up and behind where they were sitting. I couldn't see their faces and could only see the backs of their heads and shoulders. Eleanor and my wife were wearing white spring dresses, while Benjamin was wearing faded blue jeans with a white T-shirt.

The sun was setting as I peered over the field. The sky glowed pink cotton candy with a mixture of fiery reds and oranges, interwoven with small streaks of clouds on the horizon. I could picture a long dirt road that led to the house from a main road in the distance.

I saw a white vehicle in the distance. I could tell it was making its way towards the house because of the small bloom that kicked up while it was coming down the old dirt road. I saw birds flying in the sky and Olive, our Goldendoodle, lying in the grass near the front porch. As the white car sped towards the house, I felt a warmth all over my body. This sensation was much different from before. It felt like love, joy, and happiness. I felt totally immersed in the images my mind was creating.

As the car got closer and closer, my family stood up from their chairs. I could feel their anticipation. They seemed to know who was coming down the road. They knew who was returning home, but I didn't yet. It was like I had been left in the dark about the traveler. The car stopped, and the door slowly opened. I saw flip-flops touch the ground. The passenger in the car was me. I was watching myself return home.

The tears rolled down my face, but this time, I just let them go—I didn't fight them at all. I was completely open to everything my mind was creating, and it was very freeing. I watched myself walk towards the house; I was wearing board shorts, a long sleeve white shirt, sandals, and sported a crappy goatee from a few months without shaving. Best of all, the huge smile on my face felt true and honest.

I walked with a different swagger. I was light on my feet, and it reminded me of the feeling I had had when I watched Shawn walk down the aisle towards me at our wedding. She was pure beauty and focus; nothing in the world mattered but us. I finally got to the porch and joined in a huge family hug. I locked eyes with Shawn. She has these wonderful, blue-colored eyes that mesmerized me just the same way they had when I first met her.

I was home and being embraced by the ones who meant the most to me. I heard myself say, "I did it, I'm free, and I'm home." I slowly closed my eyes, and the horror film was over. When I reopened my eyes, I felt some of the weight of the world being exhaled through my nose and my mouth. My mind was at ease while the tension in my head and temples faded. The world glowed again.

I had to be committed to an inpatient facility to truly go the distance with EMDR because of how negatively the process had affected me. There was no other place I would have been able to do this treatment unless I was under round-the-clock care of nurses and doctors. I had to be in a safe place to heal because of all the damage I was doing to myself to get better. The trauma of reliving these events was just so taxing on my body and mind.

Success was only achievable for me with EMDR because of the other professionals who were there to help me heal concurrently. When I finished my extended stay at ECBH, I really felt that I had gotten my life back on track. I didn't go to ECBH to escape reality or to be away from the world. I went so that I could enjoy the reality of the world with all of my mind, body, and soul. When I started the program at ECBH, I thought I would never have another chance to get better. Maybe this was the last chance I had to get my life back. I knew I had two kids that needed a father and a wife that needed a husband. I continued EMDR with a new therapist when I returned to Key West. We worked on my war traumas and the moral atrocities associated with warfare. The traumatic events in Afghanistan hadn't impacted me as much as the sexual trauma I endured early in life, so this therapy was less painful though still exhausting.

There were a lot of people who helped me through this recovery. I gave them everything I had because I knew that if I didn't, I would have been dead within a few years. EMDR was an amazing tool for me that helped me absorb and desensitize the most traumatic moments in my life. I also worked on other traumatic events which were not as emotionally charged but had suicidal feelings wrapped within the memory.

When I left ECBH, I also had a new mission in my life. I needed to find ways to share my story. It made me happy to know my story helped others heal. There is hope and healing within my story. I wanted people to understand their options.

———

I will do whatever I can to share my life experiences. Remember, these are my life experiences. You must never try to put your life into mine. Everyone's life is hard. Life is hard, period. Everyone is living the human experience, and during this experience, there will be pain. You are not alone. There are a lot of choices for therapy. Just choose something if you feel you need it. It will help you to be vulnerable and teach you how to talk about your experiences.

I left SFUWO about a year after leaving Emerald Coast. During my last year there, I spent a lot of time in the ocean and a lot of time with my kids. I thought that I needed to take my mind off the missions and the men and to focus more on me. After the army, there would only be my family and nothing more. My kids were a pretty big challenge for me at first.

Why do I get frustrated with children? Because I am used to people following orders that are given to them. My interactions with my children have helped me to grow as a person. My kids have helped to build a stronger family bond. Parenting is a test that never ends and always comes back for more. I believe raising my children has helped me understand the meaning of life.

I truly love being a father. The happiness I receive from my children fills me completely. The lessons they learn in their youth are super important in developing who they will become later in life. I want to show love for my children and teach them lessons the best way that I can. I want my kids to always want to come back to where they were raised. I'm hopeful there will never be a time when they won't want to come home. Loving and being present for my children is what I learned while living in Key West as well as learning to love myself.

I vowed to create the family that I always wanted and needed. I know there will be hard times when raising my kids because they don't understand the world in the manner that their parents do. I must remind myself that the process of growing requires growing pains. I still have growing pains when reading to my children, but I welcome them. Sharing struggles and experiences with my kids is crucial for our growth.

I love reading to my children. I've always struggled with reading to myself, and reading out loud is even harder for me. Reading to my children reminds me of a time when I was very frustrated, but they have to realize that Shawn and I will not always be around to pick them up and put them back on their feet. I must teach them how to sometimes struggle on their own.

After being in Key West for three years, my family headed back to Fort Bragg, NC; I joined them a few months later. I was assigned to a United States Special Operations Command as a Non-Commissioned Officer in Charge of the Special Operations Joint Task Force – Bragg (SOJTF-B). I became the senior enlisted at this small unit. The unit helped train soldiers to deploy to support missions in Iraq and Afghanistan. The new role gave me some time to develop as a leader, enhance my management skills, and build on staff work. It was a remarkably interesting assignment, one in which I got a better understanding of the strategic atmosphere of the

Middle East and Central Asian States. My office was in a secure building that had no windows. It was a big change from the environment of Key West, where I spent every day outside under the sun.

While at Fort Bragg, I continued to search for ways to get my story out. I went to the human performance and wellness office at 3rd Special Forces Group Airborne. There, I learned about a new procedure that they thought might help me feel even more than rehab. I was told that there was a doctor practicing near Chicago who had developed a procedure that was really helping a lot of people with their trauma.

This is how I learned more about the Stella Center. The Stella model treats mental health challenges as injuries, not disorders. This groundbreaking procedure would soon give me great relief.

A year after my family made the move to Fort Bragg, I traveled to Chicago to visit the Stella Center. This was the recovery path that took over twenty years to navigate. The unlucky trajectory of my life ended with a lucky feeling and the absence of sadness and regret. I am extremely grateful to have some wonderful people in my life who have allowed this journey to happen. I am still unsure if it's luck, or if that's just the way life is sometimes.

My time at Emerald Coast took a lot of the sting of my childhood trauma away and provided me with many coping mechanisms, but I could still feel that something within me wasn't quite right. Sometimes, I would cry on my way to work and had to convince myself that life was still worth living, that maybe my luck would change, and that I would stop having to continually talk myself off the edge of life and death.

I went into an IV Solutions clinic in Chicago for a ketamine treatment, which was co-located with Stella. The anesthesiologist and the medical doctor explained that ketamine treatments were said to help with traumatic brain injuries. The ketamine treatments would also function as a kind of fertilizer for my brain to prepare it for the Dual Sympathetic Reset (DSR), an advanced version of the stella ganglion block injections that I would receive three days later.

The DSR is a simple, two-site injection into the side of your neck with a local anesthetic around the neck vertebrae. On each side of your neck, there is a bundle of nerves, called the stellate ganglion. This bundle of nerves is where the doctor injects the anesthetic. I received the DSR and ketamine all during the same week.

The ketamine clinic was in the basement of the building. I filled out a few forms prior to getting to Chicago that recorded my feelings of depression and suicidal ideations. A nurse walked me back to my room, prepped my skin with alcohol, and put the IV into my left arm, the very same location where I had injected myself. The nurse checked my blood pressure and heart rate. All was normal, and I was ready to receive my first dose of ketamine. The anesthesiologist drew the ketamine into a syringe, then injected it into the IV fluid bag that was connected to the tubing in my arm. Within fifteen minutes, the ketamine started to take effect— a wild experience. I was viewing and feeling the world differently. The phases of the ketamine treatment were different than anything I had ever experienced with other drugs or alcohol.

First, I felt all the pains throughout my body slowly disappear. Next, I could feel the weight of my life slipping away out of my mind. It was hard to focus on things with my eyes because the objects I looked at seemed to bend a little, kind of like the wind swirling in the Starry Night painting by Vincent van Gogh. This shiftiness was not overwhelming to me; it was just a little odd because no one had prepared me for what to expect.

The hallucination made the painting of the tree hanging in the room look as if it was kind of blowing in the wind. Then, I felt as if my mind was wandering through the cosmos—as if I was on another plane or another dimension. This felt like something that Neil Gaiman's Sandman character, Dream, would be living in and not just exploring.

On the third day, I returned to the Center for the next stage of the DSR procedure, but no ketamine. After years of therapy, countless attempts to figure out how to be healthy, getting sober, a ton of days of inpatient care, being misdiagnosed with bipolar disorder, and taking on the personal label of alcoholic, I was introduced to Dual Sympathetic Reset.

The shots made the lights come on for me. I could see the world through a much wider lens. In a way, the DSR freed the raging monster that had torn apart the cell it inhabited within my mind. The monster left the cell where it had been held against its will. It felt extremely tired. It carried a few generations of pain on its shoulders, and it was careful not to leave anything behind in the cell when it left.

That night, I truly rested.

In the following days, the procedures were absorbed into my mind, body, and soul. This internal healing happened on its own, without a therapist. At forty years old, I had thought about killing my stepfather every day for the past thirty two years, every morning as soon as my feet touched the ground.

After receiving the second DSR shot in the left side of my

neck, all the doom of the world had vanished as if a veil had been lifted from my eyes.

I received another IV infusion of ketamine in the afternoon. I walked around the city and ate dinner. I felt very calm and the fear of something bad happening was simply not present. I started to notice the poor and homeless on the streets of Chicago. I wondered if they had ever felt safe.

I went to bed around nine thirty; I felt exhausted from releasing the weight off me and from the internal battle I was waging in my ketamine trips. In the morning, my thoughts were different. I had always felt the desire to kill my stepfather, but now, for the first time in thirty two years, my desire was to live.

I forgave him for what he had done. I had tried for decades to forgive this man for what he had done to me. I felt like I had finally won. I won my life and my innocence back. I felt as if the future was more than just one more day. I knew my children would definitely have a great father and that my wife would never have to worry about losing her husband ever again.

As the treatments went on throughout the week, I needed to be alone and wander about Chicago; I needed to process this new way of thinking, this new perspective on the world. Free from the gripping past, I walked to Wrigley Field from downtown Chicago and then walked back downtown along Lake Michigan.

I saw that everything I had wanted to do in life had come true. I had gone to college, earned a master's degree, and was a Special Forces Green Beret, a husband, and a father of two awesome kids.

I also took some time to listen to music and think about

the ways my mind, body, and soul had changed. I listened to Radiohead's *OK Computer* album as I walked around the city. The song "Lucky" was the one that hit me. This song helped me complete my journey. It was perfect. I wasn't sure how, with everything that had happened in my life, my luck could change. I thought I would spend the rest of my life fighting thoughts of suicide and always feeling like I had to pull myself out of something. But that day, I felt it all fade away. It was a glorious afternoon! I couldn't imagine where destiny would take me next.

Three months after my treatments in Chicago, REZZ was playing at Red Rocks in Morrison, Colorado, on my forty-first birthday. REZZ is a female electronic dance music artist who wears spiral, light-up glasses while she performs. I traveled to Colorado on my own. I had met my guide to this special place twenty-two years earlier when we rushed Theta Xi fraternity at Purdue University.

The Red Rocks have an indescribable feeling about them. I watched as the sea of people moved together like a single being. My soul felt free. I could feel the energies of the other people inside me. Being around other humans who were all focused on one thing together was a power I learned that night. I learned that I need times like these to set my mind and body free. Some people call it "the zone," but I think it was a perfect harmony of my surroundings. REZZ played a great set, the music was loud, and the lights flashed in unison to the beat. Soon after this wonderful concert experience, I would have a very special lunch that would culminate with me being on a pretty big stage.

Three months after my birthday celebration at Red Rocks, I was on a plane again. This time, I was headed to Portland,

Oregon to sit down with the board members of TEDxPortland. I had dreamt about an opportunity like this for years. The amount of people that I could reach now was much greater than at Emerald Coast Behavioral Hospital. The ability to put my story on a bigger stage was being offered. I knew I just had to be myself and share an idea that was worth spreading to the world. My story could change people's lives, and I just needed to be authentic.

The conversation was set to take place in a local coffee shop. I flew out the day before to prepare. TEDxPortland board members were curious about how the stellate ganglion block treatments work, how the treatment changed my life, and how it should be shown to the world.

The meeting consisted of five staff members of the TEDxPortland team. I knew what the SGB treatment had done for me and my family. I recognized what my childhood was like, and how going to war had made me feel inside. I had practiced and practiced trying to explain how my world had changed because of this treatment. Finally, all eyes were on me, and I got my chance to explain how my life had improved due to this treatment.

I spoke for about five minutes explaining the rough times I had lived and how I was finally shown that my life was worth living for. I didn't feel the same doom and gloom inside my body and mind anymore. I spoke sincerely and honestly; I was straight to the point with no fluff. This was an idea worth spreading. The looks on the faces of the board members said it all. I was going to go on stage and share my story and the impact of the treatment with the world.

Ten days later, I received a welcome letter asking if I would consider being a speaker.

We would be honored to collaborate together
and deliver a TED talk on "understanding,
surviving, and re-defining trauma."

There is no better person in the world to deliver
this talk than you, Trevor.

You are an inspiration to all of us and an advocate for
PTSI innovation, growth, and well-being.

Let's empower future generations with
knowledge and tools from your experience.

Thank you for your consideration.

Five months later, I would be standing on a red X, live and in front of 3,500 people.

———

The number of hours I spent rehearsing my TEDx speech was immeasurable. I read the speech aloud from the notes on the wall word for word before standing up and doing it again. This was a new process for me, and it felt very daunting at first, thinking there was no way that I could internalize my speech. However, I knew I wouldn't be nervous if I put in the hours needed and the hard work of getting better at presenting.

The words would cross my mind throughout the day, and I would think of the audience. I mentally placed myself in the Keller Auditorium, filled the 3,500 seats with faces, and imagined all their eyes centered on me. I thought of the mental challenges that I might face during the TEDxPortland. I knew that I was going to reveal a personal story, an emotionally-charged one. I knew that line by line, I would be reliving past events, but that the audience would be living the story for the first time. I thought about the audience how this talk would impact them and how they might react to hearing my story. I was worried about stumbling over my words, losing my tempo, and not engaging the audience. I didn't fear sharing. I feared failing.

I had wished for an opportunity like this when I was in rehab, four years earlier. At rehab, I saw my story change the lives of two specific gentlemen, who had both held on to their sexual traumas for over twenty years before sharing. Both men expressed to me about how much weight had been removed from their minds and bodies by finally sharing their their own personal experiences.

I had seen what sharing my story has done for people in my past, and I was thankful for the opportunity to share some of it with the world this time. My dream was about to become a reality.

However, talking in front of people was something I had been afraid of most of my life. Army training and combat were different than the stage. I trained hard for combat; I knew I had to do the same thing for this talk. Everyone has their own anxieties, their own struggles, but practicing and drilling helps these feelings become less impactful. Reading aloud in class and during training raised my anxiety because I struggled with sounding out words. The process of building and crafting public speaking skills was daunting especially when it was something I never thought I was good at.

Practicing a ton helped me to overcome these fears. I remembered that earlier in my life, learning the material and repeating the main points out loud had helped me to get better at public speaking. While I was in Key West, I had a lot of opportunities to speak in front of students, soldiers who were attending dive school.

When I first arrived in Key West, there was so much about scuba diving that I didn't know. I would read and study the *Navy Dive Manual* to better understand the skills I needed to teach others. It was my goal to become an expert in keeping students safe.

It took about two years to become an expert in scuba diving. There was just so much information to learn. I just needed to keep trying and do my best. I had to show up every day, ready to teach and learn something new. The continuous sharing of methods of mindfulness, thinking, and behavior change helped me make the skills more concrete. I had to be able to adjust to every new student and instructor, and I had to be able to adjust my TEDx speech over time as well.

Internalizing the words was the main concept that TEDx-Portland's speaker's workshop conveyed during their two-day training. Internalizing is vastly different from memorization. This change in delivery provides the speaker with confidence and gives the audience a more "present" feel from the speaker. Gradually, my talk started to feel more like a conversation. Through hours of practice, I started to lose the anxiety I had about public speaking. I felt more excited as my worries began to fade.

Looking down at my shoes, I took a slow breath, filling my lungs and letting my arms relax. I looked at the crowd for a split-second glance, and I knew I had to say the words. I felt anxious and scared but excited about what I was about to do.

I began speaking. I felt stiff and angry, the same way I had felt for so many years. I began to think about the births of my children and was about to cry. I reached up to my forehead and took another big breath. *Keep talking, Trevor.*

I continued through the talk. I gradually relaxed, and a smirk became apparent; I felt the smile on my face. I knew that the true me was being shown to the audience. As the sentences continued to flow from my mouth, I started to feel alive. I moved through my life on the stage.

As I got closer to the finish with just a few lines to go, I felt the energy of the crowd. Then, I delivered the last lines of the talk. "I accept that bad times will reappear, but now I know they don't last. Now, joy and happiness always return."

I saw the crowd clapping, and a slow wave of the audience began standing on their feet. I had never felt that much energy. I walked offstage, and the weight of months of work slid off my shoulders.

I called Shawn right away. I cried to her; the emotions overwhelmed me. Shawn shared how proud she was of me and how vulnerable I had been. She said I was the strongest person she had ever known.

The work I put in shows that I am serious about this public speaking adventure and moving more into the next phase of my life—talking with people about trauma and healing. Making connections easily is something I was born with and have used on the streets, in college, and in the Army. Now, I am using these skills in a new arena.

I love talking and sharing with other humans. I know how important it is to have networks with others. This is what builds strong communities which can impact the lives of others. People must be able to trust what you are saying and feel that you are a genuine person.

Why does all this matter? Simply put, you are not alone in your struggles and desires to find answers to your questions. I have noticed that most of the questions I had were answered over time by me putting my head into books to study, practicing a lot, and doing some self-reflection.

Once I stopped caring about what others thought and was okay being me, I really started to get better. Getting in touch with and expressing my true feelings about my experiences was when the biggest changes occurred.

Other people will recognize aspects of my experience and hopefully relate. If this appeals to you, then please go out and talk about your experiences and attempt to seek whatever help makes the most sense to you. Crafting my story and explaining it to other people has helped me recover the most. This has worked better than any of the medications I have taken over the years. Everyone's story has value.

About two months after standing on the X in Portland, it was the hottest day on record for the planet, and we were celebrating the independence of America. My family and I decided to spend the day at Grayton Beach, twenty-five minutes from our house, a place where time seems to slow down and people are very kind.

We had recently purchased a twelve-foot paddle board. Shawn and I thought the waves wouldn't be too bad, so we decided to try it out and see how it would handle in the ocean. Driving the family car around with the board loaded on top always scares me. The feeling always takes me back to college when I had a 1969 Ford Bronco with a removable top. One night, I was driving the Bronco down a country road, and the top flew off! I constantly think this will happen again. So, I strapped the board down with two sets of tie-downs so that it was secure.

We arrived around one o'clock and the beach looked like it had thousands of people on it, the most people I'd ever seen on the beach. Big crowds of inexperienced swimmers make it hard for me to relax. I often think that people are swimming drunk, or parents are not physically capable of saving their kids. My kids were hyped by all the people and the music, and the vibe was just electric. I carried the board into the water; the waves were about two to three feet every six seconds, and the current was about one knot. These were great conditions. I got the kids onto the paddle board and pushed us all into the ocean about twenty meters out. I stayed on the back of the board and acted as an anchor and a rudder. It was great to watch my kids climb up and jump off into the water.

The kids dove for sand dollars and got to swim with a lager neck sea turtle, too. I stayed out in the ocean with Eleanor and Benjamin for the next four hours. They took breaks to eat food and drink water, but they just loved riding on the front of the paddle board like it was a bull, up and down, crashing through the waves.

I understand why people go to the beach on holidays and special occasions. Most people might only get to the beach once or twice a year, but Shawn and I saw the value in raising our kids at the beach. The beach offers us physical fitness, outdoor activities, and opportunities for family bonding. The ocean and the beach are the places my family loves to go to. I will always be thankful that we took advantage of all the time we spent boating and being together on the sand bars while we lived in Key West.

That day, I was in the ocean for five hours swimming with Shawn and our kids, Eleanor, now nine, and Benjamin, six. This time felt amazing to my heart, and the connection to my family was wonderful. It reminded me of the times my brother and I were together when we were younger, spending long days swimming and getting our feet burnt from the hot sand. I am grateful to have been able to spend a day like that with my family and friends.

The hard work to stay fit gave me the strength and energy to be able to spend this time playing with my kids. I am thankful to be a member of Miramar Beach Strength and Conditioning. The gym has always provided a space for Shawn and me to have time to ourselves, and most importantly, to keep our fitness solid. Our relationships with the other members have been incredible, and we've found like-minded people to surround ourselves with.

Later that afternoon, I was alone with Benjamin on the board, floating out in the ocean. Benjamin crossed his legs as he sat down on the board. He looked right into my eyes and said, "Daddy, I love you more than anything in the world." I am so lucky to still be here to have that moment with him. Hearing my son tell me he loved me that day made all my healing work worth it.

Later that night, Eleanor asked me if I would braid her hair. Braiding hair is something I haven't spent much time doing, but I said I would try. Eleanor sat on my lap, and I started to braid her hair. The braid was nowhere near perfect, and it took me about three minutes to complete. I tied the end of the braid, and Eleanor flipped it over her shoulder as she approached her mirror. She took a quick look at my awful work and smiled. She then returned to me and gave me the most precious kiss on my cheek and said, "I love it, Daddy, thank you."

I will remember these two moments forever. Sharing times like these is very special to me and makes me feel like I am a good father. We are growing into a strong family. Days like this are what I was hoping to achieve by moving to Florida and choosing a home near the beach. Shawn and I value the quality time spent together as a family.

Rising from the depths of my hell to finally reach the surface was painful and required a lot of hard work. I've had failures and some big wins throughout my journey so far, and you will as well. I have come to realize that taking great care of the one and only body I have is important. I had to heal my brain to allow my heart to catch up.

Throughout my journey and experiences, I have come to understand that humans truly need other humans in their lives. I encourage everyone to enjoy a live concert or some other healthy communal experience. We are meant to be surrounded by the people we love and who care about who we are inside. The people who are close to me in my life never gave up on me. This strength of others has shown me that I can conquer just about anything if I have enough time and a true friend by my side.

Some of the darkest feelings I've ever had were encompassed in this latter part of my journey. My suicidal feelings felt as if I was holding my breath deep underwater in a pool and thinking things in my life were so dark that drowning would be a better alternative than rising to the surface.

Now, imagine that second breath is the only thing that matters in the world. The urge for that breath is how I would describe addiction. I hope this visual will help you understand addiction, if no one has tried to describe it well to you. It's a tall task to try and overcome addictive tendencies, but it has gotten easier with time, practice, and encouragement from others.

If you are going to spend any time in rehab, I would encourage you to give it your all. People who don't give their recovery all their effort are a hindrance to the process and are not very helpful at all.

Please give me your truth and tell me your story. Storytelling is the easiest way to take the hurtful past and let it go. No one else can take these steps for you. I wish that you have just enough courage to start your journey. If you don't have someone in your life who will listen, then please lean on the resources at the end of this book. Release your pain from your mind and body. Only you can make that choice.

Allow yourself to be vulnerable enough to let yourself grow out of being comfortable. Learn something new and realize that you're going to suck at it at first. I had to tell myself this constantly when I first started spearfishing. Sometimes, you have to take a chance with people who are outside of your normal peer group.

Finally, there are a lot of modalities and options for you to choose from throughout your journey. It is up to you, and only you, to decide what works best for you in order to resurface from the depths of your own traumas. Seek treatments and therapies that fit your needs. There are new methods and therapies being discovered all the time that could help you on your journey. Put in the work and time, and know that healing can sometimes take many years to accomplish, but that life will always be worth living.

I want to leave you with the tools and techniques I have

used over the years to help me achieve a joyful life. I'm hopeful you can learn from my stories and that you might be able to recognize some of the pitfalls or areas you might be currently stuck in.

Bad times will not last forever, and the same goes for the good. Don't succumb to the "always happy" trap. That's just a stinking way of thinking. Being human is painful and traumatic for every single one of us. I will listen to your story and will always want to hug it out. The fire that burns inside you may feel invisible; you think no one else can see or feel it. I promise others can see it and feel it when you are around them. You must show your fire to the world. Together, we can defeat monsters.

Difficult stories show us that monsters exist,
but they also show us monsters
can be defeated.

ACKNOWLEDGEMENTS

For every single person who offered to walk with me through the journey of recovery, I will be indebted to you forever. For everyone who showed me that there was still love inside me and to those who helped me believe in myself again. Jess Forsythe and Mike Kenna. Paul Toolan and Jared Nichols. Brian Soderquist and Dick Khuel.

To the men of the Theta Xi Fraternity (Theta Chapter) at Purdue University, you helped me through some of the challenging times of my life. YITB.

To all the men of the 151st LRSD (2004-2006), you are my band of brothers. The leaders and men of this unit built the base for me to recognize and foster within myself the strength to become the best soldier and Green Beret that I could be. Pat Keane, Jordan Stone, Clark Strickland, John Piper, Sean Eaken, and Mike Vogt.

To the Special Forces Regiment, always continue to take care of each other—we are all we got. There is no helicopter thirty seconds out to help us; no one is coming to save us. Caring for each other must be within our new purpose and mission. Call, talk, and listen to our brothers; this truly really makes a difference. Ron Jillard, Benjamin Tabberer, Brian Santos, Justin Grant, Dave Murphy, Sean J. Rogers, Nick Lavery, and Chris Cathers.

The men of ODA 3431 ... I love all of you! You all have a place in my spirit that I will never forget.

Marshall McGurk, you are the best dive buddy I ever had. You showed up and took care of me as a leader, a man, a brother, and a father. Thank you for being a mentor to me and so many other Green Berets. You are one of the *boys* I would follow back into combat if you ever asked. You are going to be an amazing father. I am sorry for the loss of your brother. DE OPPRESSO LIBER.

Eddie Rojas, I appreciate your love of life, family, and the ocean. You encouraged me to find a love for being on the ocean and truly loving family and friends no matter what. Your genuine love for my children, I will never forget. While at SFUWO, you always had my back and you never judged me after I quit drinking. I love you, brother.

Dave Withrow, you are the most genuine friend that I have ever had in my life. The hours of talking, traveling, and dancing have impacted my life forever. Thank you for showing me the power of Red Rocks. I completely understand why it is your happy place. Learning about Magic: The Gathering, playing in real life gets me out of my comfort zone and makes me do something that I suck at that has been powerful. You gave me the strength to continue to write, allowing me to explore my vision and to help me dream big.

For the doctors and therapists who never gave up, your work and the commitment to helping people achieve a smile again and find self-love will always be needed. Dr. Roy Deal and Dr. Eugene Lipov, you are the superheroes of the world.

For the researchers gathering scientific data on the impacts of abuse, war, and stress, thank you; I know that much of this work goes unnoticed. Continue to do your magnificent work—our world needs true and accurate data.

Tara McGuire, you are a marvelous editor, and The Self Publishing Agency, your guidance and knowledge of publishing a book were outstanding.

To everyone who thinks that they are alone in their suffering ... please know you are not alone and that your story matters and must be heard. Please continue to share. This allows you to get out of the self-made prison that you have built.

To my wife, Shawn, the strongest person I've ever met ... I love you.

ABOUT THE AUTHOR

TREVOR A. BEAMAN is an active-duty US Army Special Forces Green Beret, father, and husband. He grew up near Chicago, attended Purdue University, and is a multi-combat tour veteran. Trevor has survived many years of traumatic experiences including early childhood abuse, substance abuse, war, and the loss of loved ones. He speaks and writes about the journey of recovery and has contributed to suicide awareness. Mr. Beaman currently lives near the ocean in Santa Rosa Beach, Florida.

RESOURCES

988 Suicide & Crisis Lifeline - Call. Text. Chat.
https://988lifeline.org/

Green Beret Foundation
https://greenberetfoundation.org

Mission 22
https://mission22.com

Brothers Keeper Veteran Foundation
https://bkvf.org

Rape, Abuse & Incest National Network (RAINN)
https://www.rainn.org

Have a problem with alcohol? Alcoholics Anonymous
https://www.aa.org

Having a problem with narcotics? Narcotics Anonymous
https://www.na.org

National Human Trafficking Hotline—1 (888) 373-7888

National Sexual Assault Hotline—1 (800) 656-4673
(1-800-656-HOPE).

There are many programs in your local area. Look for
inpatient and outpatient services that suit your needs.

www.ingramcontent.com/pod-product-compliance
Lightning Source LLC
Chambersburg PA
CBHW020250130626
46549CB00005B/2160